Ryan Post

JESUS PEOPLE

Communities Formed
By The Beatitudes

ENDORSEMENTS

"Living the Sermon on The Mount by the empowering presence of the indwelling Spirit requires the willingness to endure hardship and embrace adversity in order to experience enlargement. As Rowan Williams said, 'Discipleship is a state of being.' In other words it is ontological. It is far more about who we are than it is about some technique. In a technocratic culture, where *how-to's* are in vogue, Ryan Post offers us a return to the profound and simple formational call of Jesus, which is 'Follow Me,' and invites us to take one step at a time in doing so. The most pressing questions we can ask as followers of Jesus are, *Where is Jesus going?* and *Are we going with Him?* Ryan offers us wisdom for both answering these questions and responding to the summons of Jesus and then taking the necessary steps."

Dr. Mark J. Chironna

Lead Pastor, Church on the Living Edge, Longwood, Florida

Author of *The Dead Prophets Society: The Significance of Prophetic Function in the 21st Century*

"History shows how surpassingly difficult it is for Christians not to forget Christ. All too often, in the name of Christianity or the truth, and in defense of our way of life, we Christians prove false to Jesus. So we need constant reminding that we are called by the Spirit to live the same cross-bearing, enemy-loving, God-fearing life that he lived. Thankfully, Ryan Post's book does precisely that, directing our attention not to Jesus as we imagine him but to Jesus as the Gospels present him to us."

Dr. Chris E. W. Green

Professor of Public Theology, Southeastern University, Lakeland, Florida

Author of *Surprised by God: How and Why What We Think about the Divine Matters*

"To believe in Jesus is to believe the words of Jesus in such a way that God's people embody God's radiant light in a weary world. With robust Biblical scholarship and a loving pastoral heart, Ryan Post unpacks Jesus' call to a 'holy we' instead of a 'holy me.' When we live in communities that are formed by the Beatitudes the world will look and see Jesus People."

Tara Beth Leach

Pastor and Author of *Radiant Church* and *Emboldened*

"*Jesus People* is a book for God's people. Ryan Post carefully and pastorally leads us through the prophetic blessings bestowed upon the people of the kingdom of God. Taking us deep into the language of the Beatitudes, Post draws out deep truths illustrated by his own experience as a Jesus person and as a pastor. This book is what we need today to grow as followers of Jesus and engage God's good but broken world as the people of Jesus."

Derek Vreeland

Discipleship Pastor, Word of Life Church, St. Joseph, Missouri

Author of *By the Way: Getting Serious About Following Jesus*

"It's easy to despair about the state of Christianity. Just look at what scrolls across your news feed, but maybe we're looking in the wrong place. *Jesus People* gives us a glimpse into God's new world already emerging. This is a sweeping and thorough narrative of what breaks in when real people decide to follow the way of Jesus, together. It will move you from despair to dreaming about the Kingdom possibilities. Ryan Post has given us something of a manifesto for being the broken but beautiful community we know can exist. This is the pathway forward for our times!"

Dan White Jr

Author of *Love Over Fear* and Co-Author of *The Church as Movement*

Developer with The V3 Movement

Jesus People: Communities Formed by the Beatitudes

www.ryanpost.com

Published by Muscadine Press

ISBN: 978-0-578-82512-0

Cover Design: Augusto Avila www.studioavila.com

Formatting: www.dragonrealmpress.com

Editing: Beth Gaede

For Carrie

my loving wife & trusty hiking partner

TABLE OF CONTENTS

CHAPTER ONE

HIKING THE JESUS TRAIL

With the help of our Lord God, let us diligently beware henceforth of giving men a false confidence by telling them that if once they will have been baptized in Christ, no matter how they will live in their faith, they will arrive at eternal salvation.

—Augustine of Hippo, *Faith and Works*

North America is a place where people have absorbed just enough Christianity to inoculate them against the contagion by the real thing. We believe that the church can be a major means of conversion, detoxification, and inculcation of the practices required to be Christian in a world that thinks it already is.

—Stanley Hauerwas and William Willimon, *Resident Aliens*

One of the most prominent geological features around the region of Galilee is a towering cliff known as Mount Arbel. Located just north of the ancient city of Tiberias, it offers a breathtaking view of the Sea of Galilee and the surrounding territory.

Several years ago, I was leading a pilgrimage tour in Israel. One morning we planned to hike the trail down Mount Arbel. We drove to the top of the mountain, got out of our vehicles, and took some time to enjoy the scenery. A few moments later our trail guide gathered us together and gave us some coaching. Warning us of the possible dangers ahead, she instructed us to stay close together, to be aware of our surroundings, and to move at a slow and careful pace. None of us had any idea what we were about to experience. About twenty minutes into the hike she led us to a steep cliff face, explaining that we would now climb down the cliff together.

Without any safety gear. Or landing mats. Or medics on hand.

We were incredulous! As the trip leader, I was petrified that one of us would lose footing and fall to certain death (and by "one of us," I mean *me* especially). To be fair, several in the group were invigorated about the challenge ahead. But more than a few were quite panic-stricken. Yet, there was no turning back.

The descent took nearly all morning. With only a steel cable to grab, we meticulously inched our way down the treacherous cliff while carefully placing our feet along the rocks below. Once we all landed safely on level ground, everyone breathed a huge sigh of relief. We continued the remainder of the hike reveling in our accomplishment. It was an experience we will all remember for the rest of our lives. And we did it together.

Hiking is not simply about getting from point A to point B. It is not solely about arriving at the destination as quickly as possible. Obviously, the destination is important. No one would ever want to get permanently stranded out in the middle of the wilderness. But a hike is also about the journey itself. I will never forget that trek down Mount Arbel—not only the hazardous climb down the cliff, but also the gorgeous views. The distinct fauna and flora. The ancient caves. The aroma of the fresh mountain air. The entire hike is an adventure from beginning to end. All along the way, there are valuable lessons to be learned and unforgettable experiences to be shared.

"I AM THE WAY"

Using one of his famous metaphors, Jesus declares of himself: "I am the way" (John 14:6). He doesn't say, "I will point the way." Or "Here, let me draw you a map." Jesus *is* the way. The path. The hiking trail.

As such, we must not see Jesus simply as a means to an end. Too often, the gospel is presented as if only the destination is significant. Particularly among evangelicals, the call to faith often goes something like this: "Believe that Jesus is Lord, ask him to forgive your sins, and invite him into your heart, so that you can be saved and go to heaven when you die." There is often little or no emphasis on the ongoing adventure of becoming his actual apprentice for life.

Imagine someone staring at a trailhead declaring, "I believe that this trail leads from point A to point B," and then expecting to be suddenly transported to the other end. Of course, *believing that* the trail will lead to the desired location is essential. But at some point, one must actually begin walking. In other words, if I believe that a trail will lead me where I want to go, then it will be undeniable and observable as I begin hiking. Otherwise, I will remain stationary regardless of what I believe to be true about the trail.

Likewise, *believing that* Jesus is Lord is not the same thing as *embarking on* the Jesus way.[1] Trails are meant to be

---

[1] For a helpful and thorough exploration on the meaning of the New Testament use of the term "believe" (*pisteuo*) and how it

followed. And Jesus intends for his apprentices to trust him and to practice his teachings. Isn't that what apprentices do after all?

One of his statements near the end of the Sermon on the Mount makes this abundantly clear (it also makes many modern Christians nervous): "Not everyone who says to me, 'Lord, Lord,' will enter the kingdom of heaven, but only the one who does the will of my Father in heaven" (Matthew 7:21). Jesus explicitly reveals that the kingdom of heaven is reserved for those who do the Father's will. Not merely for those who give mental assent to the right doctrines. Nor for those who have prayed a "sinner's prayer" or even have a rich devotional life. But for those who *do the Father's will*. To put it differently, only those who hike the Jesus way will experience the life of heaven.

"THE KINGDOM OF HEAVEN"

Now, before we can move forward, we must gain clarity on what is meant by Jesus' term "kingdom of heaven." It is an expression that he uses frequently throughout the gospel accounts. In Matthew's gospel alone the term shows up

---

relates to salvation (e.g. John 3:16), see *Salvation by Allegiance Alone* by Matthew Bates (Ada, MI: Baker Academic, 2017).

twenty-nine times, while Mark and Luke use the term "kingdom of God." But the two phrases are theologically identical.

Many Christians assume the phrase "kingdom of heaven" refers to a future place or reality that will be revealed upon Jesus' return, when he will set everything right for all eternity. And this is certainly one of the implications of this phrase. The New Testament clearly teaches that there is a final destination in which all will be made new (Revelation 21 is a particularly beautiful, poetic description).

However, when Jesus uses *kingdom* language, frequently he indicates that the kingdom is also a *present* reality that was already beginning to break forth into the world upon his arrival. For example, he once explains to a group of Pharisees: "The kingdom of God can't be detected by visible signs. You won't be able to say, 'Here it is!' or 'It's over there!' For the kingdom of God is already among you" (Luke 17:20b-21 NLT).

The kingdom of God, therefore, is both a future and present reality in which things have come (and are coming) into alignment with God's vision for human society and all of creation. And this reign has already been inaugurated with the arrival of God's Son and Israel's Messiah, Jesus

Christ. Jesus launches his public ministry with the following announcement: "The time is fulfilled, and the kingdom of God has come near; repent, and believe in the good news" (Mark 1:15). Immediately following this announcement Jesus begins his ministry, traveling throughout the region of Galilee healing the sick and casting out demons. Each of these acts is a demonstration of the *reign of heaven* on earth. They are signs to the crowds that a new era has come (and is coming) through the person of Jesus Christ.

But these miracles are also accompanied by frequent periods of teaching. In fact, Jesus seems to place a particularly strong emphasis on his teaching ministry. While his miracles are almost always a spontaneous response to the needs of others, he often seems to intentionally plan and carve out time for teaching and instruction.[2] In other words, the miracles and healings are tangible demonstrations to confirm and draw attention to his overall message that the reign of God is breaking forth into the world. It's as if Jesus is saying, "I've demonstrated for you that the kingdom of God is in your midst.

---

[2] For a few examples, see Matthew 5:1-2, 11:1, 13:1-3; Mark 1:21, 4:1, 6:2, 6:6, 10:1; Luke 4:15, 13:22, 19:47, 21:37-38; John 7:14ff, 8:2; Acts 1:3.

Therefore, let me now teach you how to align your lives under God's reign."

Here is where our hiking analogy fails us (as all analogies ultimately do), because trails and destinations are two separate things. While they connect to one another, once I arrive at my final destination, I have no further use for the trail. However, according to Jesus and the entire witness of the New Testament, heaven is not only a final destination that we shall experience in some future age. He emphatically declares that God's new world is already beginning to emerge into the present for those who are following the Jesus way. This is why Jesus taught us to pray: "Your kingdom come. Your will be done, on earth as it is in heaven" (Matthew 7:10).

To be sure, this heaven-and-earth alignment won't be fully consummated until his return. In the meantime, there will always be some level of struggle for those who participate in God's work in this broken and damaged world. But regardless, even now Christ's followers are called to be the first fruits of the coming harvest giving the world a taste of what is to come.[3] Or to use a modern

---

[3] See 2 Thessalonians 2:13, James 1:18, and Revelation 14:4.

analogy, we are to be the *preview* of the *coming attraction* of the life we will enjoy when all is made right.

And we fulfill this calling as we gather together and learn to become practitioners of the Jesus way, heeding his words and putting them into practice. This is what it means to be "Christian." The gospel invitation that permeates the entire New Testament is to begin the journey of becoming nothing less than an imitator of Jesus Christ.

"CONVERSION" WITHOUT APPRENTICESHIP

What troubles me is that much of the modern evangelical movement in America does not seem to grasp the priority of the call of apprenticeship to Christ. Rather than teaching people to obey everything Jesus has commanded us,[4] many churches seem to treat discipleship as an optional accessory, choosing instead to focus on selling the basic "conversion" package (afterlife insurance included).

In their book *Renovation of the Church*, Kent Carlson and Mike Lueken tell the story of the church they co-pastored in Folsom, California. Oak Hills Church was

---

[4] See Matthew 28:20.

planted in the early 1980s and began as an attractional, seeker-driven church that was growing rapidly. Their Sunday morning productions were entertaining and engaging, and people were responding at a staggering rate. But along the way the leadership of the church began to perceive a certain shallowness in their discipleship efforts that was being reflected in the life of their congregation. Though they were offering discipleship classes, the overwhelming majority of their energy and resources centered around the Sunday morning production designed primarily to elicit decisions for Christ.

Over time they began to realize that though their methodology was producing impressive measurable results, it was also communicating that the ongoing journey of learning to imitate Christ was secondary. What really mattered was making an initial decision. Even though the pastors would have never consciously endorsed this idea, this was the message they were unintentionally communicating through the approaches they were using.

They arrived at the realization that methodology is not value-neutral. Our methods reflect and influence the content of our message. If we are using techniques that cater to people's consumeristic, *what's-in-it-for-me* instinct, we are yielding to values that are diametrically opposed to the call of Christ. Eventually the leadership of Oak Hills Church guided their church in a slow and painful (but healthy) shift away from the attractional model. And it all began with an honest assessment of the condition of their own spiritual health: "We had grown the church, but we were not more like Jesus. Growing the church did not require that we be like Jesus. It wasn't as though we were blatantly sinning and trying to hide it. But the leadership energy required in a larger church and the adrenaline rush of outward success gradually substituted for authentic experiences with God. The enthusiastic buzz in our church validated what we were doing."[5]

These are sobering thoughts. A church may be growing and expanding, but if the spiritual health of its leaders is languishing, perhaps it is the indirect result of being confused about the nature of our mission. Imitating Christ was, is, and always will be the objective. When we shift our target away from apprenticeship and instead focus on winning initial converts, we may fill churches and calm anxieties, but we will not produce practitioners of the Jesus way. Numerous recent studies have revealed that the moral standards and behavior of those who profess to be born-

---

[5] Kent Carlson and Mike Lueken, *Renovation of the Church* (Downers Grove, IL: IVP Books, 2011), 40.

again evangelical Christians are virtually indistinguishable from that of non-believers.[6] To put it simply, the twenty-first century church is experiencing nothing less than an appalling crisis of disobedience among those who self-identify as evangelical Christians. This is the spoiled fruit of a church culture that divorces apprenticeship from conversion.

Teaching people how to become a Christian is easy. It's efficient. It's measurable. Teaching people to become Christian is none of those things. This is the tough, hard, unglamorous work of discipleship. It demands bold leaders who are not seduced by the acclaim of statistical success and who care for nothing more than making apprentices of the Jesus way. One can become a Christian in an instant. But becoming Christian is a lifelong expedition. Becoming Christian entails becoming a practitioner of peace, forgiveness, mercy, justice, and enemy-love. This requires fortitude, self-denial, and patience. It comes through pain, adversity, and the

---

[6] For a concise summary, see Ronald Sider's book, *The Scandal of the Evangelical Conscience* (Ada, MI: Baker Books, 2005).

empowerment of the Holy Spirit through spiritual disciplines.[7]

Yet this process of apprenticeship is something that church leaders like me simply cannot measure or quantify. We can count lots of things: attendance, offerings, small group involvement, and follow-up cards. But we cannot measure the actual progress of one who is growing in love for God and others. We can observe it, of course. But we cannot chart it on a spreadsheet.

And as long as church leaders focus on the "measurables" of church life, we will have a tendency to marginalize that which cannot be measured. To take it even further, it is possible to be doing quite well in the "measurables" category ("Attendance is booming, and our small group ministry is multiplying!"), and yet utterly fail at our commission to become imitators of Christ and lead others in the same.

Of course, there may be other valid reasons for keeping track of church metrics. But once we begin to equate "measurable results" with faithfulness to the gospel, we

---

[7] For a primer on the spiritual disciplines, I highly recommend Richard Foster's *Celebration of Discipline* (San Francisco: HarperOne, 2018) as well as Dallas Willard's *The Spirit of the Disciplines* (San Francisco: HarperOne, 2009).

will inevitably warp our message and compromise our prophetic witness. This is something Jesus was never willing to do.

JESUS AND THE CROWDS

Throughout the story of Jesus recorded by the gospel authors, as he goes about proclaiming and demonstrating the arrival of God's kingdom, crowds are flocking to him from every direction. News of his miracles is spreading, and his popularity is sky-rocketing.

But what strikes me is that Jesus never allows the size or the enthusiasm of the crowds to steer the content of his message. There is nothing inherently wrong with enthusiastic crowds, of course. But it seems that often during these moments of large-scale visibility, Jesus gives his most polarizing teaching and sayings.[8] Regardless of his growing fame and influence, he faithfully declares the message of his Father, even when it causes the crowds to desert him.[9] Here's a glaring example of this devotion: "When the crowds were increasing, he began to say, 'This generation is an evil generation; it asks for a sign, but no

---

[8] See Matthew 5:48; Luke 9:37-43; 14:25-33 for a few examples.

[9] See John 6:66.

sign will be given to it except the sign of Jonah'" (Luke 11:29).

Statements like these really cut against the grain of the predominant philosophy of the modern church-growth movement. For many church leaders, accumulating a large following is seen as a primary goal. *Attract as many people as you can, generate momentum, figure out what they are looking for in a church, exceed their expectations, show them how their lives will improve, avoid anything that would make them feel awkward, and then tell them to invite their friends so next Sunday there will be an even bigger crowd.*

If Jesus were following church-growth conventions, he'd say, "Alright, the crowd is coming, so let's put our best foot forward. Let's capitalize on this momentum!" But in this case Jesus gives a strong, confrontational word. He's essentially saying: "Why are you here? Are you looking for some religious carnival? What did you come out to see?" Jesus is more interested in the condition of people's hearts than he is with the size of the crowd.

Acquiring a sizable following is not evidence of faithful ministry. Again, there is nothing intrinsically wrong with assembling a large crowd. But it must not be taken as an automatic sign of success. It may be evidence of a well-executed production, a charismatic personality, or an appealing program. But it's not necessarily evidence that the kingdom of heaven is advancing. The evidence that God's kingdom is expanding is simply that people are hearing the instruction of Jesus and they are obeying it. When people are beginning to look like Jesus, love like Jesus, and sacrifice for others like Jesus, the reign of heaven is moving forward.

Church leaders must abandon the endless pursuit of statistical validation. If we are constantly chasing whatever we think will make our churches grow bigger and faster, then the question that guides our decision-making will inevitably be "*What works?*" But throughout his letters, the apostle Paul doesn't seem remotely interested in growth strategies and attractional techniques. In fact, he never even provides a single comment on these matters. It is quite apparent that Paul's enduring question is "*How can we follow well in the footsteps of Christ?*"

We are not called to be great or significant. We are only called to be faithful. And when Christians get serious about living faithfully according to the teachings of Christ, history has shown that the impact on the wider society can be rather remarkable.

According to the available evidence in our possession, the growth of the Christian movement in the first 270 years of its existence was not the product of strategic growth models and vetted marketing strategies. It just *happened*. The leaders of early Christianity never wrote about ways to systematize the expansion of the Christian movement. They simply believed that as local communities of believers lived out radical obedience to the Lordship of Christ, growth would be an inevitable result. The substance will produce the effect. But they didn't see visible expansion as something they must control or manufacture.

Their role was to be properly formed in the way of Christ. They recognized that this process of formation cannot be rushed or expedited. They felt no pressure to produce quantifiable results. They weren't enchanted with measurable statistics. They only cared about living out their faith with pure fidelity and then passing it on to others who would do the same.

In the midst of our conventional outreach strategies and sleek structures and processes, we need to ask, what is the quality of our Christian witness to our culture? Whether our churches are excelling in attaining numerical goals, are we being formed by the Sermon on the Mount? Are we growing in our love for our enemies? Are we being known and recognized for being people of mercy? For being peacemakers? For being patient during hardship? If we are interested in authentic discipleship, these are the essential questions we must be willing to embrace.

THE BEATITUDES

As Jesus launches his public ministry, he begins recruiting disciples, teaching in synagogues, curing sicknesses, delivering demoniacs, and proclaiming his earth-shaking announcement: "Repent, for the kingdom of heaven has come near" (Matthew 4:17). And shortly after his ministry commences, Jesus gives his most famous address, the Sermon on the Mount.[10]

Somewhere around the northern shore of the Sea of Galilee, a massive crowd begins to gather around Jesus. News has been spreading about the miracles he has been performing. When Jesus sees that this huge crowd is assembling, he begins to climb a nearby mountain. Finding a suitable place, he sits down to signify that he is beginning to teach. And his newly chosen disciples form an inner ring around him.

Now we must pause for a moment and consider the sequence. Jesus is baptized, then spends forty days in the

---

[10] See Matthew 5-7.

wilderness, and now sits atop a mountain in order to teach his apprentices before a multitude of people gathered at the base of the mountain.

We can identify here a striking resemblance to the *Exodus* story. Many centuries earlier, God delivered the Israelites from slavery in Egypt by miraculously leading them across the Red Sea. They would go on to spend the next forty years in the wilderness of Sinai. In the midst of that experience, Moses ascends up Mount Sinai and receives the Law from God and delivers it to the gathered masses below. So just as Israel passed through the waters, journeyed through the wilderness, and received the Law from Yahweh at the foot of a mountain, Jesus re-creates the Exodus sequence. By doing so, he identifies himself as the one who will embody the mission of Israel and carry it through to completion.[11]

So when Jesus sits atop this mountain with the disciples assembled around him, he is re-enacting the Sinai experience. Just as Moses received the Law from Yahweh and gave it to the twelve tribes from the summit of Sinai, Jesus is re-forming Israel around himself and giving his disciples a new Torah that we call the Sermon on the

---

[11] See Genesis 12:3 and Isaiah 49:6.

Mount. According to New Testament scholar Scot McKnight, "Jesus is teaching the new Law as the new Moses for the new people of God."[12]

Hence, this is no ordinary sermon from Jesus. This is the most complete and most important sermon he ever preached. It is his manifesto for human society. And for those of us who call ourselves followers of Jesus Christ, we must pay special attention to this famous discourse. We must not ignore it, soften it, or domesticate it in any way.

It is impossible to really understand Jesus apart from the Sermon on the Mount. The Sermon on the Mount can be seen as the constitution of the kingdom of God. It is his *Gettysburg Address*. His "I *Have a Dream*" speech. Through this magnificent sermon, Jesus is showing the world God's true intention for human life and society. He is revealing his vision for a new culture of *Jesus people*.

And at the very beginning of the Sermon on the Mount we find eight prophetic "blessings" (Latin: *beatus*) spoken from the mouth of Jesus. They are known as the *Beatitudes*. If the Sermon on the Mount is the constitution of the kingdom of God, the Beatitudes compose the preamble.

---

[12] Scot McKnight, *The Sermon on the Mount Commentary* (Grand Rapids, MI: Zondervan, 2013), 24.

As we will see, these eight statements are not to be seen as charming, common sense platitudes. Each of them is meant to come across as shocking, disturbing, and counter-intuitive. Yet collectively, they capture Jesus' vision for life with God. In fact, together they actually provide a concise summary of Jesus' own life, teaching, death, and resurrection. Jesus didn't just teach the Beatitudes. He embodied the Beatitudes. And for those who are following him, the Beatitudes are the stones that pave the Jesus way. Each of them perfectly depicts God's agenda for God's people *and* how that agenda will be carried out. According to scholar N. T. Wright: "When God wants to change the world, he doesn't send in the tanks. He sends in the meek, the mourners, those who are hungry and thirsty for God's justice, the peacemakers."[13]

So throughout the remainder of this book, we will examine each of these eight Beatitudes not only in light of how we must live, but especially in regards to how local churches are called to approach our God-given vocation.

Blessed are the poor in spirit, for theirs is the kingdom of heaven.

---

[13] N.T. Wright, *Simply Jesus* (San Francisco: HarperOne, 2011), 218.

> Blessed are those who mourn, for they will be comforted.
> Blessed are the meek, for they will inherit the earth.
> Blessed are those who hunger and thirst for righteousness, for they will be filled.
> Blessed are the merciful, for they will receive mercy.
> Blessed are the pure in heart, for they will see God.
> Blessed are the peacemakers, for they will be called children of God.
> Blessed are those who are persecuted for righteousness' sake, for theirs is the kingdom of heaven (Matthew 5:3-10).

I want to personally challenge you to commit each of these statements to memory. Use them daily in prayer. Internalize them with deep reflection. Allow these words to be sown deeply into the soil of your heart. Let them begin to dislodge your hidden assumptions that prevent the kingdom from taking root. And over time, you will discover that your life will begin to blossom with the ripe fruit of God's Spirit.

REFLECTION QUESTIONS
CHAPTER ONE

1. In what specific ways does the journey of discipleship compare with the experience of hiking a trail? How does this hiking metaphor interact with any views of discipleship you may have held in the past?
2. What are some common misconceptions people may have regarding Jesus' term "kingdom of heaven?" What are some possible negative ramifications of these misunderstandings? Why is it essential that we properly comprehend the meaning of this all-important term?
3. Do you agree with the notion that much of the twenty-first century church has not faithfully adhered to the mission of making apprentices of Jesus? If so, what are some of the indicators? Also, where can you identify some encouraging signs that the message of authentic discipleship is indeed taking root?
4. What do you think about the idea of measuring success as it relates to local church life? Is it possible? What are some signs that authentic discipleship is happening?
5. In what specific area of your life is your own commitment to being a disciple of Christ currently making demands upon your life?
6. In what way(s) do you sense the Holy Spirit may be calling your local faith community into deeper discipleship?

CHAPTER TWO
THE SPIRITUALLY DESTITUTE

Blessed are the spiritual zeros—the spiritually bankrupt, deprived and deficient, the spiritual beggars, those without a wisp of "religion"—when the kingdom of the heavens comes upon them.

—Dallas Willard, *The Divine Conspiracy*

After two centuries of mounting anticipation, the announcement is finally made that the long-awaited kingdom of God is beginning to break forth among humankind. Jesus begins to travel throughout the region of Galilee proclaiming the good news to the people that this kingdom has "come near" and is now "among [them]."[1] But what will this kingdom look like? And how will it come? The popular Jewish assumptions that were hovering over these questions would need to be addressed and corrected. So Jesus takes a seat on a small boulder. His disciples are gathered in front of him with a large crowd assembled at the bottom of the mountain. And Jesus begins to deliver the greatest sermon ever preached.

---

[1] See Mark 1:15 and Luke 17:21.

At the very beginning, he gives a famous collection of eight statements we call the "Beatitudes." Contrary to popular understanding, the Beatitudes are not advice or instruction. They are not commands. Nor are they formulas for success. The Beatitudes are simply announcements. Through these eight statements, Jesus identifies the *kinds* of people who are going to find the arrival of this kingdom to be good news.

Each one of them begins with the word "blessed," a translation of the ancient Greek word *makarios*. But *makarios* is saturated with meaning that cannot be adequately captured with a single English word. In classical Greek thought, the term was associated with *the life of the gods*. So in Christian usage, we might refer to the *blessed ones* of the Beatitudes as those who are candidates to become "partakers of the divine nature" (2 Peter 2:4). In other words, that they are *blessed* means they will share in the very life of God.

Each of the Beatitudes ooze out of Jesus' entire life and teachings. His death and resurrection perfectly compress and embody the Beatitudes. And together, they describe the company of those who are hiking the Jesus trail: the spiritually destitute, the mourners, the meek, those who crave for things to be made right, the merciful, the pure-hearted, the peacemakers, and those who suffer for the right reasons.

Through these eight iconic blessings, Jesus announces that these are the ones who will experience the divine life. But they are also the ones *through* whom the kingdom will grow and expand. Though the world typically avoids and tramples upon these kinds of people, they are the very ones through whom Jesus will advance his reign—people just like himself.

Let's examine the first one: "Blessed are the poor in spirit, for theirs is the kingdom of heaven" (Matthew 5:3).

PENES OR PTOCHOS?

Two Greek words can be translated as the English word "poor." The first one, *penes*, has to do with people who are struggling but still able to sustain themselves. These peasants work as day laborers, toiling in the fields and living hand-to-mouth. Throughout the ancient world, the majority of human society fell into this category. They were the vast labor force that undergirded an economy pillaged by the powerful. These people surely weren't saving any extra money, and they had no chance for upward mobility in the face of an exorbitant tax system that sucked all of the profits out of their production. But they were still able to provide for their own basic daily necessities.

Yet, the Greek word translated "poor" in this Beatitude is actually the word *ptochos*. It refers to the totally destitute. These are people who have no capability for self-sufficiency whatsoever. Their lives are hanging by the very edge of existence. The homeless wanderer cut off from his family. The penniless widow without a safety net. The crippled beggar on the side of the road. The *ptochoi* are those who are so poverty-stricken that without the aid of others their survival would be utterly hopeless.

The focus of this particular Beatitude is the "*ptochoi* in spirit." Jesus is referring to the spiritually destitute. These spiritual beggars understand that they cannot afford the luxury of arrogant pretense and are willing to go to the most desperate lengths to receive their sustenance from God alone. The ptochoi in spirit are ones who are cloaked in humility and under no delusion of self-reliance. They fully grasp the reality that apart from the ongoing stream of God's mercy nothing can satisfy their parched souls.

Jesus declares that such people are blessed because they are recipients of the greatest treasure of all—the kingdom of God. But why is this the case? Because only those who are spiritually destitute are capable of walking the Jesus way of forgiveness, peacemaking, and patient endurance of persecution. One cannot follow Jesus on this narrow way unless one is willing to embrace a life of self-denial. These are the people through whom the kingdom of heaven grows and expands on the earth. The Christian life requires an ongoing poverty of spirit. Once we begin to buy into the illusion of self-sufficiency, spiritual growth is stifled and the kingdom will pass us by.

It may be pointed out that Luke's version of this Beatitude is slightly different: "Blessed are you who are poor, for yours is the kingdom of God" (Luke 6:20). Here, the emphasis seems to be placed on economic lack rather than spiritual condition. However, in the ancient world these were very often two sides of the same coin. Though rulers and empires changed hands, the relentless pressure on the peasant class was constant, sometimes mounting to a nearly unbearable level. By and large, it was because the poor had been so beaten down by life in a society that was beyond their capacity to influence that they were particularly primed for the inbreaking of God's kingdom. They simply had nothing to lose. And for many, their spiritual condition was a mirror image of their economic desperation.

Century after century, the Jewish peasantry had been crying out to God for relief and deliverance. Many of them had given up hope altogether. But now Jesus finally arrives, and with the very first sentence of his most important sermon, he turns the world upside-down. "How blessed are those who are destitute in spirit, because the kingdom from heaven belongs to them!" (Matthew 5:3 ISV). While this blessing certainly has future implications, Jesus would go on to demonstrate repeatedly that it has already begun to take effect.

Even a cursory review of the gospel accounts reveals that these are exactly the kinds of people who are beneficiaries of some of Jesus' finest work. In a world dominated by the wealthy and powerful elite, Jesus chooses to work on the fringes of society, focusing on the weak, the powerless, and the discarded.

BLIND BARTIMAEUS

One of my favorite illustrations of this Beatitude involves a blind beggar named Bartimaeus.[2] On his last stop on his journey to Jerusalem, Jesus makes a brief appearance in the

---

[2] See Mark 10:46-52.

nearby city of Jericho. A multitude of his followers from the surrounding regions has also swarmed upon the city. The common assumption held by this crowd is that within the next few days this Messiah will make a bold entrance into Jerusalem, usurp control of the temple, seize and consolidate power, violently drive out Israel's enemies, and successfully lead a new Jewish revolution.[3]

Anticipation is building. The atmosphere is electric. As Jesus walks down the main thoroughfare of Jericho, people are piling on top of one another just to catch a glimpse of this famous prophet. And sitting by the roadside is a typical *ptochos* named Bartimaeus. Though he cannot see anything, Bartimaeus certainly senses the unusual frenzy around him. Once he realizes that Jesus of Nazareth is passing by, he begins to cry out, "Jesus, Son of David, have mercy on me!" When the people around him attempt to silence him, he raises his voice even louder: "Son of David, have mercy on me!"

Now for a moment, imagine what it might be like to be in Jesus' position. A festive parade has spontaneously

---

[3] Within a few days they will celebrate Jesus' entry into Jerusalem by waving palm branches and shouting "Hosanna to the Son of David!" These actions signify a cry for political revolution and victory over their enemies.

gathered to celebrate *your* arrival. Hordes of people are chanting *your* name. Momentum is at a fevered pitch. The spotlight has never been brighter. Perhaps the natural proclivity of most mortal human beings in a moment like this would be to soak up all of the applause and adulation with proud self-satisfaction.

And yet when Jesus hears the plea of this feeble beggar, he stops dead in his tracks—but not simply because Bartimaeus is a blind beggar. In all likelihood, there would have been plenty of beggars lining the roads as news spread about the arrival of this huge influx of visitors.

It is Bartimaeus' *poverty of spirit* that arrests Jesus' attention. Bartimaeus is under no delusion of grandeur. He has a clear grasp of his desperate need for the mercy of Christ. And ignoring the disdain of those who seek to quiet him, he pleads for mercy, his desperation pouring from the core of his being. Such bold faith often flows from the heart of broken people like Bartimaeus and attracts the attention of God. So Jesus freezes in place and calls the man forward. Leaving behind his cloak, which he uses for collecting money, Bartimaeus carefully approaches him. Then Jesus asks him a fascinating question: "What do you want me to do for you?"

Bartimaeus doesn't beat around the bush. "My teacher, let me see again." Jesus proclaims, "Go; your faith has made you well."

And I love how the story concludes: "Immediately he regained his sight and *followed him on the way*"[4] "The way" is an expression loaded with double-meaning. It is the early Christian term for what we call Christianity.

A PAGE-BY-PAGE PATTERN

This story represents a consistent pattern in Jesus' ministry that can be found on virtually every page of the gospel writings. From Herod's prison, John the Baptist sends messengers to Jesus asking him if he is indeed the Messiah.[5] Jesus' response is a summary of his ministry, his acts of power and compassion delivering the least of society—the blind, the lame, the lepers, the deaf, and the impoverished—from their desperate state.

Even many who are stigmatized because of their own scandalous decisions— adulterers, tax collectors, prostitutes, centurions, and Samaritans—find a welcoming embrace in Jesus' kingdom. While they are all despised by

---

[4] Italics added.
[5] See Luke 7:18-23.

the religious elite, the gospel narratives are packed with examples of notorious sinners like these experiencing transformation in their encounters with Jesus.

These *ptochoi* in spirit have no impressive feats of religious devotion to stand upon. Nor do they have anything to offer Jesus in return. Jesus gains no strategic advantage by befriending these people. In fact, he reaps nothing but scorn and suspicion by identifying with the likes of sinners, tax collectors, and the infirmed. But there is something about a heart of humble desperation that God simply cannot refuse. God delights in those who recognize the sheer hopelessness of their condition outside of divine mercy. Because they are emptied of self-delusion, God can pour into them the very life of heaven.

Perhaps Jesus' mother is the quintessential example of one who lives with an ongoing poverty of spirit. Mary does not have any extraordinary traits that would distinguish her on the social ladder of importance. She's a simple girl of modest means living in a relatively nondescript village. But suddenly an angel visits her, announcing that she will miraculously conceive a baby who shall be called the "Son of the Most High" and will inherit the throne of David.[6]

---

[6] See Luke 1:26-38.

Knowing that this news will somehow turn her life upside-down in a multiplicity of ways, she humbly responds, "Let it be with me according to your word" (Luke 1:38).

Years later, she exhibits this same spiritual posture during a marriage feast in Cana. After informing Jesus about the lack of wine, Mary tells the servants at the wedding, "Do whatever he tells you" (John 2:5). Notice how similar her instructions are to the response she gave the angel years before. The life of one who walks with an ongoing poverty of spirit is always characterized by an unassuming receptivity to the will of God. Such a life opens the door for God's deep, transforming work in the world.

SAM

Sam attends our church along with her mom and dad. She is roughly around the same age as I am. She loves Jesus with all of her heart. He is the center of her life.

Sam is mentally impaired and functions on the cognitive level of a five-year-old. Although she has had to deal with considerable pain and sickness throughout her life, she is full of joy every time I see her. She can barely read or write, but her parents read to her from the Bible every day. When it comes to matters of faith, Sam understands things on a fairly simple level.

She has been taking art classes for roughly ten years. One day she decided to paint a small canvas with a beautiful depiction of the cross and the crown of thorns. As she was cleaning her brushes, her mother asked her about what motivated her to create the painting. Sam replied, "Jesus told me to." When she was asked who she created the painting for, her response was, "I'm not sure yet."

Almost a year later, the first time she ever saw me, she told her mother, "It's him. He's the one I painted it for. Jesus showed me."

Sam's painting is one the most special gifts I have ever received from a church member and sits on the bookshelf in my office. Every morning as I begin my day with prayer, at some point I slowly and thoughtfully pray through the Beatitudes. And often when I pray the first Beatitude I gaze at Sam's painting: "Blessed are the poor in spirit, for theirs is the kingdom of heaven."

As I slowly recite these words, I not only fix my eyes on the cross and the thorns. In particular, I often contemplate the precious person who painted that cross. Her painting reminds me that God's kingdom has not only come *for* people like Sam. It especially comes *through* people like Sam. God loves to manifest God's beauty and glory through those who are often overlooked and discarded.

Sam will probably never deliver a masterpiece sermon or publish a ground-breaking biblical commentary. But God is using her in magnificent ways to make an immeasurable impact on the lives of those around her.

THE CHURCH OF THE POOR IN SPIRIT

We live in a society of superstardom that seeks to glorify the grandiose and showcase the spectacular. Therefore, we tend to notice people with impressive gifts and abilities and elevate them, because we believe we can gain some benefit through them.

However, Jesus is in the habit of highlighting people whom everyone else ignores. Once, when his disciples ask about "greatness" in the kingdom of heaven, Jesus places a little child in front of them, saying, "Whoever becomes humble like this child is the greatest in the kingdom of heaven. Whoever welcomes one such child in my name welcomes me" (Matthew 18:4-5). Though children were commonly devalued and disregarded in ancient culture,

Jesus holds them up as an example his apprentices must learn from.

In another story he is sitting near the temple treasury as wealthy people are depositing large sums of money into the receptacle. But when a poor widow drops in two copper coins (worth the equivalent of a penny), Jesus calls his disciples over and draws attention to her sacrifice, saying, "Truly I tell you, this poor widow has put in more than all those who are contributing to the treasury" (Matthew 12:43).

Later that same week as he is dining at Simon's house, a sinful woman enters uninvited and anoints Jesus' feet with costly perfume. While everyone in the house is horrified, Jesus proclaims, "Truly I tell you, wherever the good news is proclaimed in the whole world, what she has done will be told in remembrance of her" (Mark 14:9).[7]

In the midst of a culture of celebrity worship, *Jesus people* must remember that the kingdom of heaven is tailor-made for simple, ordinary people. But if we are not careful, we can slip right into the worldly pattern of giving exclusive applause and attention to those in our churches who have "star power."

---

[7] See also Luke 7:36-50.

A few years ago I was sitting in a church leadership conference along with hundreds of other pastors and church leaders. The speaker explained that if we wanted to grow our churches, we must put people on the platform who represent excellence in every fashion. We were encouraged to utilize musicians and singers who were young, sleek, talented, and trendy in dress style. *If this is what our consumeristic culture expects, we must logically give it to them in order to increase the appeal of our churches*. I suspect this speaker was only verbalizing a common assumption among many church leaders.

If Jesus had operated with this mentality, he would have never enlisted fishermen as his disciples. Now certainly, I don't advocate that we start handing microphones to people who are completely tone-deaf. We should, of course, utilize people in the way God has gifted them. I also don't advise that we purposely exclude people from platform ministry precisely *because* they are young, sleek, talented, and trendy.

What I am proposing is that we allow the first Beatitude to shape the way we approach ministry. If Jesus, in the first sentence of his most important sermon, draws attention to the *blessed-ness* of the poor in spirit, we must carry out our ministry in light of this great truth. We must have the courage to evaluate our practices and ask hard questions. *Who do we celebrate? Who do we showcase? What stories do we tell? Who do we invite and make room for? Who might we be tempted to overlook and disregard? To whom do we give our undivided attention?*

Churches formed by the first Beatitude refuse to prioritize appearance, youth, and talent over humility, faithfulness, and sacrifice. Whether or not a person has impressive outward giftings, considerable wealth, or powerful influence, what truly captures God's attention is one who is poor in spirit. Often these people may not be outwardly remarkable. But they can teach us how to cultivate a heart that reflects God's vision for the world.

REFLECTION QUESTIONS
CHAPTER TWO

1. Where can you identify examples of the first Beatitude at work in the life and ministry of Jesus?
2. What does it mean to be "poor in spirit?" Who are some people that come to mind when you think of this spiritual quality?
3. Why do you think this particular Beatitude is listed first? What relationship does this first Beatitude have with the other seven (if any)?
4. What makes this Beatitude so counter-intuitive, both in Jesus' day and in our own times?
5. How might this Beatitude be challenging you right now on a personal level?
6. In your local faith community, in what creative ways might this first Beatitude give shape to your communal practices together?

CHAPTER THREE
THE MOURNERS

Until we learn to lament, we have nothing to say to most of the world.

—Michael Card, *A Sacred Sorrow*

For over half a millennium, the Jewish world had been haunted by the overwhelming anguish of losing their kingdom, their freedom, and their dignity. After experiencing invasion and exile at the hands of the Babylonians in 587 BCE, their ongoing history had been shaped by the oppressive rule of foreign powers and domestic dictators (other than a brief respite following the Maccabean revolt, 167 to 160 BCE).

During these tumultuous times, the prophets pointed to the impending arrival of God's ultimate deliverance. They periodically spoke of a coming *anointed one* who would restore the kingdom, administer justice, establish eternal rule over all, and bring total redemption to God's people.[1] Conceptions varied regarding what this savior-

---

[1] See Isaiah 9:6-7, Jeremiah 23:5-6, Daniel 7:13-14 for a few examples.

king would be like. But from one generation to the next, the Jews clung to this *messianic* hope.

However, by the first century many Jews were living in despair and disillusionment. The vicious Romans were now in power, staining their land with the blood of Jewish revolutionaries. The temple system had become terribly corrupt. And the crippling tax burden on the common people had virtually extinguished any hope of social advancement. The Jewish world that Christ was born into was defined by subjugation, exploitation, and a crushing sense of loss and defeat.

It is in *this* context that Jesus now sits before a vast multitude of Jewish peasants gathered from regions throughout Palestine as he makes this bold and subversive announcement: "Blessed are those who mourn, for they will be comforted" (Matthew 5:4).

As Jesus begins to describe the nature of God's kingdom that is being launched with his arrival, he declares that this era of deep sorrow that God's people have been enduring is coming to an end. He is proclaiming that deliverance is finally arriving for the hurting people of Israel as well as for the entire world and that it will somehow come through him and the movement he is initiating. This is the background of the second Beatitude.

In order to transpose the meaning of this Beatitude into our own context, perhaps we should explore the terms used in the passage's original language. Typically when we come across the word "mourn" we tend to narrow its meaning and associate it with only the type of sorrow that accompanies death. Of course, this Beatitude does include mourning of this kind. And Jesus' resurrection surely provides us with the comforting assurance that death has been overcome for those who are in Christ.

However, the underlying Greek word (*penthos*) encompasses a broad scope of sadness. On a personal level, it can include the sorrow of losing one's job, receiving a devastating medical diagnosis, experiencing a miscarriage, suffering abuse, and many other losses. But it can also apply to the collective grief and distress that may visit entire communities. Whether individually or communally, whenever people are experiencing intense sorrow of any kind, God's heart is stirred.

The Greek term for "comforted" here is *parakaleo*. It is the combination of two words: *para* ("alongside of; in the presence of") and *kaleo* ("to call"). Joined together, the term actually connotes the idea of an *encounter* with one who brings comfort. Elsewhere, Jesus uses a related word (*parakletos*) to refer to the Holy Spirit.[2] Therefore we might paraphrase this Beatitude this way: *Blessed are those who are living with deep sorrow and grief, for they will encounter One who will bring comfort.*

While grief is always unpleasant, it can also serve a healthy purpose. Grief has a way of melting away our self-delusions of security and control. It reveals to us the reality of our powerlessness. In doing so, it actually carves out space in one's soul to be filled with deep, lasting comfort and joy. This can be an excruciating process, to be sure. But for those who are open, God promises to fill that void in beautiful, unanticipated ways.

Those who never face grief or pain have little capacity for experiencing the richness of God's goodness. It is the hard work of grief that actually creates the void in one's soul that is necessary to encounter God in a deeper way. It also sows within us the seeds of compassion. Compassion literally means "shared suffering." It is a deep mystery, but God has so designed human beings that grief, though necessary, can be *shared*. If one has never encountered suffering it can be difficult to enter into the pain of others,

---

[2] See John 14:26.

because there is no well of experience from which to draw a natural flow of empathy.

But those who have suffered significantly can relate to the emotional burden, and therefore gain the inherent resources that can enable them to share the pain of a brother or sister. My burden becomes unbearable if I try to carry it all by myself. But when I am in a community of trusted friends who love me, believe in me, and are willing to share my pain, their companionship lessens the weight I must carry.

CULTURE OF DENIAL

The sharing of suffering is one way in which the gathered church becomes indispensable. Yet, this can only happen once we are willing to become transparent with one another. And unfortunately, transparency is not a hallmark of American society. After all, we have inscribed *the pursuit of happiness* into our Constitution, essentially making it into a cultural virtue. Therefore, we tend to be ashamed of our sadness. Just a brief stroll around social media will reveal that Americans are often in the habit of projecting an image of happiness regardless of what may actually be going on underneath the surface. For whatever reason, we tend to hide our pain like virtually nothing else.

The greater tragedy is that in many church environments we have unwittingly catered to this tendency and have created an environment that encourages a cheap, artificial facade of happiness. When people enter into our gatherings carrying emotional pain we often see problems that need to be fixed rather than people who need our supportive presence. As a result, the hurting members of our congregations become further isolated in their pain. If our worship gatherings suggest that glee is the only acceptable emotion, people can feel an inherent sense of shame over their sadness. Thus, churchgoers will often feel compelled to paint a smile on their faces before they arrive on Sunday mornings. As long as this remains the status quo, we are wasting critical opportunities for discipleship.

At least part of the problem is that many American preachers have become nothing more than purveyors of a pop psychology of happiness. We have taken the rich theology of the cross and we have traded it in for a shallow brand of inspirational Christianity. And eventually many people recognize it for the cheap imitation that it is and simply walk away from it. We must leave this thinned, watered-down version of Christianity behind.

This necessary step requires that we must be willing to slow down the pace of our lives and ministries in order to give real attention to one another. Rather than instinctively trying to "fix" people from afar, we must incarnate God's love to one another by willingly entering into one another's pain. Paul instructs us to "rejoice with those who rejoice and weep with those who weep" (Romans 12:15 ESV). This image of weeping implies making ourselves truly present to one another. Such compassion that actually costs us something. We need more than answers when we suffer. We need one another.

In their wonderful book, *Slow Church*, authors C. Christopher Smith and John Pattison write: "It's easy to lob advice and judgment when a friend's marriage is falling apart. It's more complex, and more demanding, to sit down with the couple, to listen, to work slowly and conversationally toward healing, to celebrate reconciliation or to grieve a divorce."[3] We certainly cannot give this level of personal commitment to every person we know. We have to recognize our limitations as finite beings. It will require the work of the entire faith community. Also, relational depth does not materialize

---

[3] C. Christopher Smith and John Pattison, *Slow Church* (Downers Grove, IL: IVP Books, 2014), 87.

instantly. It is cultivated over a lengthy period of time. But this is what cruciform relationships look like. As we embody compassion within our communities, we become carriers of God's comforting presence to one another.

One of the fundamental shifts we must make is in our understanding of local churches: they are not called to be the "happiest place in town." We are to be havens of authenticity. If there is any place where one should feel the freedom to be honest, it ought to be in the company of the crucified. Apprentices of Jesus have no need for pretense, because we understand that our value and identity come solely from the love of God that pours from Calvary, not from anyone else's opinion or assessment. This is what provides the foundation for authenticity. But it must originate from within one's own relationship with God. More than anything else, God desires honesty from us. God can handle our grief, our pain, our disappointment, even our rage. What saddens God is when we either hide these emotions or pretend they don't exist.

AUTHENTICITY WITH GOD

The story of Jacob at the stream of Peniel is one of the most eccentric stories in the entire Hebrew canon. He is traveling with his family and servants on his way to meet his brother Esau. At sunset he sends them along with his possessions across a stream, leaving Jacob alone. That night a mysterious man suddenly emerges and begins to wrestle with him until dawn. Here is how the episode is recorded in Genesis 32:

> When the man saw that he could not overpower him, he touched the socket of Jacob's hip so that his hip was wrenched as he wrestled with the man. Then the man said, "Let me go, for it is daybreak." But Jacob replied, "I will not let you go unless you bless me." The man asked him, "What is your name?" "Jacob," he answered. Then the man said, "Your name will no longer be Jacob, but Israel, because you have struggled with God and with humans and have overcome." Jacob said, "Please tell me your name." But he replied, "Why do you ask my name?" Then he blessed him there. So Jacob called the place Peniel, saying, "It is because I saw God face to face, and yet my life was spared" (Genesis 32:25-30 NIV).

There are so many curious aspects to this story. For one thing, there doesn't seem to be any particular event that triggers this spontaneous wrestling match. This strange man just suddenly appears and begins grappling with Jacob. What makes it even more bizarre is that this man somehow turns out to be none other than God! Jacob declares, "I have seen God face to face." And yet, the account also mentions that the man could not prevail against Jacob. That seems odd. I would assume that if he could dislocate Jacob's hip just by the mere touch of his hand, he could have pinned him instantly. And yet, we are told that the man could not overpower Jacob.

This peculiar story illustrates a profound truth about the relationship that God wants to share with us. Let me explain it this way. My oldest child is my son Carson. Every so often, Carson and I will have a spur-of-the-moment wrestling match on the living room floor, with the fate of the entire world hanging in the balance. One moment I might gain the upper hand and place him in the dreaded figure-four leg lock. The next moment, he reverses the momentum and puts me in an unforgiving sleeper hold. But for fifteen minutes or so we will struggle back and forth until both of us are exhausted.

Now here is the reality. If I wanted to do so, I could pin young Carson fairly easily and end the match in just a few seconds. But that would defeat the entire purpose of our wrestling. First, he needs to release some energy, and I certainly need the exercise. But more importantly, it's a *bonding* experience. As Carson and I are tussling around on the living room rug, our relationship is being strengthened.

I get the impression that this is similar to what we see happening in this famous biblical event. Jacob is wrestling with God into a deeper, richer relationship. And as a result, God proudly changes Jacob's name to *Israel*, a Hebrew name meaning "to contend with God." And hereafter, Jacob's descendants will be known as the *Israelites*—ones who wrestle with God. Now certainly, there can be a negative connotation of this meaning. For example, throughout the biblical narrative we do find Israel often wrestling with God due to stubbornness and sin. But on the other hand, this passage also reveals a positive side to wrestling with God. After all, it is *God* who proudly confers this name upon Jacob's descendants. The willingness to wrestle with God is the identifying mark of those who belong to God, because in wrestling with God, our faith grows and our character is developed.

PERMISSION TO LAMENT

So let me state my point very plainly: *God wants our honesty.* God can handle your prayers of grief, frustration, and anger. The biblical term for this prayer is *lament.* Throughout the Bible, one of the trademarks of many of our heroes of the faith is the audacity to take God to the mat, to contend with God. The psalmists frequently exhibit this raw honesty by offering prayers of lament. Here is a representative example attributed to the sons of Korah from Psalm 44:

> Rouse yourself! Why do you sleep, O Lord?
> Awake, do not cast us off forever!
> Why do you hide your face?
> Why do you forget our affliction and oppression?
> For we sink down to the dust; our bodies cling to the ground.
> Rise up, come to our help.
> Redeem us for the sake of your steadfast love (Psalm 44:23-26).

Jeremiah was also a fluent speaker of the language of lament. Here is one of his many expressions of grief and exasperation before God:

> Why is my pain unceasing, my wound incurable, refusing to be healed? Truly, you are to me like a deceitful brook, like waters that fail (Jeremiah 15:18).

We would probably not adapt these lines for the typical contemporary worship song, but such language is common throughout our scriptures. Biblical figures like David, Job, and Habakkuk had the nerve to pour out their laments before God, often conveying clear traces of weariness and anger with God.

Yet, God does not take offense at their honest expressions of pain. God actually welcomes this authentic prayer. Why else would we find so many prayers of lament enshrined in the Bible? Of all things, prayer is the appropriate practice through which we must bring our unvarnished emotions before God. As the story of the early life of David demonstrates, when we are willing to journey through the arid desert of lament, we actually discover a hidden oasis of intimacy with God.

Regrettably, lament is not a common word in our modern vocabulary. But it is a spiritual practice that we desperately need to recover. When the people of God fail to lament, we lose our capacity to share the pain of a broken world. Yes, there is a time to smile and laugh. But there is also a time to weep and grieve.

PRAYING THE PSALMS

One of the practices we can implement to help us find this balance in a daily rhythm is praying the psalms. To be transparent, for most of my life I have not really loved the Book of Psalms. I suppose it has something to do with my ambivalence towards poetry (I prefer prose). So when it comes to scripture, I have gravitated towards other biblical genres.

But a few years ago I came to the realization that I was confused about the purpose of the psalms. They are not primarily meant for reading or study. Instead, we *pray* the psalms. The Book of Psalms is, after all, an ancient Jewish prayer book. Like other devout Jews, Jesus himself would have memorized and prayed through the psalms as a spiritual discipline throughout his life.

We see an example of this at his crucifixion. From the cross he cries out, “My God, my God, why have you forsaken me?” (Matthew 27:46).[4] This is a direct quote from the first line of Psalm 22. Jesus is adopting the common Jewish practice of quoting the first line of a psalm to represent the rest of the psalm. Therefore, he is connecting his experience not only to that single verse but to the entire psalm. As we work our way through Psalm 22, we can identify parallels to Jesus’ experience on the cross:

> All who see me mock at me; they make mouths at me, they shake their heads…I am poured out like water, and all my bones are out of joint; my heart is like wax; it is melted within my breast…they divide my clothes among themselves, and for my clothing they cast lots (Psalm 22:7, 14, 18).

But around the middle of the psalm the tone begins to change. The psalmist shifts the focus from the pain and opposition to the eventual victorious outcome that God will bring. Here is the beautiful way that Psalm 22 concludes:

---

[4] See also Psalm 22:1.

> All the ends of the earth shall remember and turn to the LORD; and all the families of the nations shall worship before him.
>
> For dominion belongs to the LORD, and he rules over the nations.
>
> To him, indeed, shall all who sleep in the earth bow down; before him shall bow all who go down to the dust, and I shall live for him.
>
> Posterity will serve him; future generations will be told about the Lord, and proclaim his deliverance to a people yet unborn, saying that he has done it. (Psalm 22:27-31).

As Jesus is hanging on the cross, bearing the weight of the world on his back, he is drawing strength through his prayerful reflection of Psalm 22. In the midst of the excruciating pain, he is reminding himself of what is being accomplished—that ultimate deliverance will come through his sacrifice. By reflecting on this psalm, his resolve is being reinforced. He is meditating on the truth that his death will not be in vain. But the only reason Jesus was able to do this is that he had memorized and been praying through this psalm his entire life.

Several years ago I began engaging in the ancient practice of daily praying through the psalms. There are 150 psalms and 365 days in a year. On the first day of every year, I pray through the first psalm. Then I continue praying through one psalm a day (in order). On the 151st day of the year, I start over. If I will do this every day for an entire year, I will have prayed through the entire Book of Psalms roughly two-and-a-half times.

Of course, you will notice that the psalms tend to vary in tone significantly. Some of the psalms are celebratory and uplifting. Others are rather gloomy and lamentful. But I don't pick which psalm I will pray based on my mood that day. Brian Zahnd writes, "We pray the psalms, not to express what we feel, but to learn to feel what they express."[5]

Our individualistic culture has formed us to believe that something is worth doing only so long as we can gain some clear, personal benefit from it. Therefore, for me to pray through a psalm that I don't emotionally connect with in a given moment may feel like a waste of time. But this attitude is the product of a self-centered approach to prayer. Even if I may not be able to identify a reason to

---

[5] Brian Zahnd, *Water to Wine* (St. Joseph, MO: Spello Press, 2016), 78.

lament within my own personal world, I know members in the church I serve who are going through an intense season of pain. I have brothers and sisters all over the globe who are encountering trials of all kinds. It is essential for me to solidify myself with them and enter into their grief.

Therefore, I have learned to take each psalm as it comes. Regardless of how I feel on any particular day, I pray through the psalm for that day. If it is a psalm of rejoicing, then I rejoice. If it is a psalm of pain and grief, then I enter into the throne room of God and engage in the hard work of lamentation God's people must do. I do this because even on my worst day, there is something to rejoice over. And even on my happiest day, if I will just open my eyes and look around, within a few moments I will find reasons to grieve.

JESUS AND LAMENT

If for no other purpose, we embrace the practice of lament because we are disciples of the "Man of Sorrows." Jesus, being "the exact imprint of God's very being,"[6] reveals to us that God does not stand aloof to our pain and suffering.

---

[6] See Hebrews 1:3.

As Jesus constantly encountered and healed the sick, the blind, and the lame, he never related to these people or their needs with emotional detachment. Again and again, he was moved with compassion. A few days after the death of Lazarus, his grieving sister, Mary, goes out to meet Jesus. Here is what follows in John 11: "When Jesus saw her weeping, and the Jews who came with her also weeping, he was greatly disturbed in spirit and deeply moved. He said, 'Where have you laid him?' They said to him, 'Lord, come and see.' Jesus began to weep" (John 11:33-35).

It would have been understandable if Jesus had no emotional reaction whatsoever to Lazarus' death. After all, he knew he was going to raise Lazarus from the dead. However, despite knowing the outcome, Jesus is moved to tears by the emotional pain expressed by these hurting people. In this encounter, Jesus reveals to us what God is like. God does not callously shrug at the pain of the world. God dives into our pain. As Jesus stretched out his arms on the hard wood of the cross, he was submerged in a sea of opposition, suffering, and hatred. It was his "baptism of suffering."[7] Crying out, "My God, my God, why have you forsaken me," he lovingly entered into the worst possible

---

[7] See Mark 10:38-39.

feelings of abandonment and anguish that any human being could ever experience.

And this is an essential part of our gospel message. We must understand that we can't just live in the constant mode of Easter Sunday. After all, it is the suffering and sorrow of death and burial that leads to the gracious surprise of resurrection. Even though our final destiny is one of eternal celebration, the Christian life is not just about smiles, cheerfulness, and good feelings. Each of us will experience seasons throughout our lives in which we will bear excruciating sorrow, and it will seem as though God is totally absent.

But through Good Friday and Holy Saturday we arrive at Easter Sunday. And that requires that we know how to lament. Because in doing so, space is being carved into our souls that God fully intends to fill with eternal goodness, blessing, and joy.

REFLECTION QUESTIONS
CHAPTER THREE

1. In what ways does Jesus' own death on the cross speak into the human experience of suffering?
2. In your own experiences with pain and suffering, how have you encountered the comfort of God's Spirit?
3. In these painful experiences, can you remember specific people who have helped you carry the burden?
4. Have you noticed ways in which your own encounters with suffering have helped you to emotionally connect with others who are suffering in a similar fashion?
5. How can local churches work to become places of healing for the broken? Within your own context, can you identify any possible adjustments that can be made?
6. In this season of your life, how might God be speaking to you personally through this Beatitude?

CHAPTER FOUR
THE MEEK

If your life is motivated by your ambition to leave a legacy, what you'll probably leave as a legacy is ambition.

—Rich Mullins, from a radio interview[1]

Thousands of travelers from every direction swarm the hill country on the northwestern coast of the Sea of Galilee. They have accumulated and gathered to learn at the feet of this young prophet from Nazareth whose fame is ever-expanding. And right at the beginning of this seminal sermon, Jesus reveals the third Beatitude: "Blessed are the meek, for they will inherit the earth" (Matthew 5:5).

This is the only Beatitude that is a direct quotation from the Hebrew scriptures—from the middle of Psalm 37:

> Yet a little while, and the wicked will be no more; though you look diligently for their place, they will not be there.

---

[1] According to a family friend, this quote originated from an interview with Rich Mullins conducted at a radio station in Nashville, Tennessee.

> But *the meek shall inherit the land*, and delight themselves in abundant prosperity (Psalm 37:10-11[2]).

Notice that the word "land" is used here rather than "earth," alluding to the "Promised Land" of Israel. Throughout the calamitous centuries following the Babylonian invasion, the Jewish people clung to the hope of once again dwelling in the land God had promised them, unencumbered by the rule of foreign powers.

Therefore, when Jesus makes this announcement, he is striking a familiar chord with his audience, the vast majority of whom are Jewish peasants who have been suffering under the heavy weight of Roman occupation. He is drawing upon a rich history of Jewish hope and expectation anchored to this ancient promise. *Everything will be turned upside-down. The era of inheritance is near.*

Once we understand the context of this Beatitude, it is not difficult to see what makes it so subversive. Stationed amid the crowd that day would have probably been a small contingent of Roman soldiers, positioned to monitor this spontaneous assembly. I can imagine that upon hearing these words these soldiers might have rolled their eyes,

---

[2] Italics added.

smirking at one another. Rome ruled most of the world known to Westerners, an enormous territory that stretched from Spain to Syria. The Romans didn't *inherit* the earth. They just took it. They conquered the earth through aggression and military might. They were able to maintain power by establishing efficient systems of roads, currency, and government. But most importantly, the Romans had assembled the most powerful military force in the world. They were the dominant superpower of the age, operating under the principle that the world is seized by the strong and gobbled up by the greedy. Yet, within earshot of Roman soldiers, Jesus announces to this multitude of powerless peasants, "Blessed are the meek, for they will inherit the earth."

To *inherit* something is different from *taking*, *seizing*, and *conquering*. An inheritance is received, usually through an established relationship. If you inherit something from your parents, you did nothing to earn it. It has been graciously bequeathed to you simply because you are fortunate enough to have been their child. And Jesus declares that the meek are the ones who will inherit the earth.

MEEKNESS, NOT WEAKNESS

The notion that *meekness* is synonymous with *weakness* is terribly mistaken. The word "meek" in this Beatitude is translated from the Greek word *praus*. It was commonly used to describe the nature of a tamed animal. For example, one might imagine a wild stallion that has been captured and trained so that it might carry a rider or be fed by the hand of a child. The horse still has all of its strength and swiftness. It hasn't lost a bit of its capacity. But its raw power has been brought under control and focused for a purpose. This is what *meekness* means. Indeed, it is the opposite of weakness. It is strength brought under control.

Jesus is referring to the tamed strength of those who are capable of absorbing the blow of unjust oppression, without taking vengeance into their own hands. They understand that the earth belongs to God, and God's agenda will ultimately prevail. Therefore, to be *praus* is not to be passively resigned to an inglorious fate. It is to have confident trust that God's final word will ultimately satisfy those who hike the Jesus trail. One who is meek will not *seize* what is meant to be *inherited*. The kingdom of God does not advance by conquest but through God's vindication of those who trust the Calvary way.

In the first century, God could have used other means to revolutionize human society. Tiberius Caesar was the emperor of Rome and perhaps the most powerful person on the planet. At the snap of his fingers, Caesar could bring quick and pervasive change to the Western world. The Roman Senate was perhaps the most influential political body on earth and could significantly alter human life through policies and laws. The Roman army was perhaps the most formidable military force in existence and able to coerce entire nations into conformity with Roman policy. God could have chosen to use other power brokers in the region, such as Herod Antipas, Pontius Pilate, or Joseph ben Caiaphas—leaders with robust power, wealth, and social influence. By relying on shrewdness and clout, they also could get things accomplished rather quickly and efficiently.

But instead, when God launches his kingdom project, God raises up Jesus of Nazareth who willingly embraces a humble, self-sacrificial death on Calvary. And it is Jesus, the perfect embodiment of meekness, who God exalts as ruler of all. "I will make the nations your *inheritance*, the ends of the earth your possession" (Psalm 2:8 NIV, emphasis mine).

THE WAY OF SELF-DENIAL

Christ crucified is the quintessential example of meekness in two important and inseparable ways. Though he had the power to rescue himself and summon twelve legions of angels to annihilate his enemies, Jesus submitted himself to the will of his Father. Stretching out his arms on the cross, he prayed, "Father, forgive them; for they do not know what they are doing" (Luke 23:34). This is meekness displayed in its purest form. It is the utter denial of self-interest in subservience to the will of God for the sake of others.

It is impossible to follow the way of Christ while simultaneously choosing the path of prestige and power. Power can take many forms: skills, charm, charisma, money, connections, intellectual ability, political sway, and theological acumen. Obviously, none of these are evil. But each can be strategically employed to manipulate others for one's own selfish pursuits. One of the greatest barriers to the spread of God's kingdom is the preoccupation with the advancement of our own counterfeit kingdoms.

The Calvary way is the antithesis of a life driven by unrestrained ambition. By exemplifying meekness on the cross, Jesus is giving us an example of how to go about our mission. We are not called to be glamourous superstars for Jesus. We are called to be faithful servants who take up our cross and follow him. As long as we allow ambition to steer the wheel, we may be saying all of the right things, but we are not living in true apprenticeship to Christ who has called us to lay down our lives for our neighbor.

Most of my fellow church leaders understand the temptation to draw a feeling of self-worth from our own ministry achievements. Surely God does summon us to accomplish great things. After all, churches must be planted, ministries must be launched, sermons must be preached, books must be written, and knowledge must be gained and shared. Ambition is not inherently evil, so long as it is channeled properly. But when our own performance becomes the source of our sense of value and identity, we have veered off the Calvary path.

Typically, an obsession with achievement becomes evident in the way we relate to the people around us. The primary indicator that I may be trying to generate my own sense of self-worth is when I begin feeding off of other people. I can do this by either seeking the attention and acclaim of others or by finding other ministers and churches to habitually criticize and even hold in contempt.

In either case, I am treating other people as objects to be used for my own self-interest. This is the way of Caiaphas, rather than the way of Christ. Henri Nouwen writes: "The true challenge is to make service to our neighbor the manifestation and celebration of our total and undivided service to God. Only when all of our service finds its source and goal in God can we be free from the desire for power and proceed to serve our neighbors for their sake and not our own."[3]

This freedom can be discovered through the ongoing practices of solitude, silence, and formational prayer.[4] When engaged daily, these disciplines can help keep us rooted in the loving presence of God, which is to be our sole source of worth and identity. Embracing a regular practice of unhurried solitude gives the Holy Spirit space and time to lovingly purify our ambitions. It is *being with God* that fuels and sustains *doing for God*.

Aside from these disciplines, it may also be helpful for us to embrace a practice of obscurity. Pastors and other leaders are accustomed to being the public face of churches

---

[3] Henri Nouwen, *The Selfless Way of Christ* (Maryknoll, NY: Orbis Books, 2007), 65.
[4] I've written about these practices in *Healthy Prayer: Integrating Structure, Silence, and Spontaneity* (Redding, CA: NewType Publishing), 2018.

and ministries. It may be beneficial to periodically distance ourselves from public exposure, which often fuels personal ambition. This can include a short annual season away from pulpit ministry and limiting one's social media consumption and output. Perhaps we can begin a generous habit of serving and giving to other churches and ministries while intentionally remaining anonymous, resisting the urge to work it into a sermon illustration.

Whatever it takes, we must learn to become content with obscurity and have the courage to face the question: *Who am I apart from the applause and recognition of others?* For the leader driven by ambition, anonymity is medicine for the soul.

THE WAY OF PATIENT TRUST

Though the powers and principalities would orchestrate Jesus' death to make him look small, insignificant, and shameful, he surrendered himself to the agenda of his Father, trusting that God would vindicate him and inaugurate the kingdom he gave his life to bring about. Therefore, he willingly embraced the cross he was given. In doing so, he was embodying one of his famous parables: "The kingdom of heaven is like a mustard seed that someone took and sowed in his field; it is the smallest of all the seeds, but when it has grown it is the greatest of shrubs and becomes a tree, so that the birds of the air come and make nests in its branches" (Matthew 13:32-32).

On Good Friday, Jesus of Nazareth is brutally murdered before a public gathering outside of the city walls of Jerusalem. His followers have scattered in fear. His closest friends are crushed. To any observer it appears that this grassroots movement that began in the hills of Galilee will now fizzle out and die. The Roman Empire has once again snuffed the torch of yet another would-be revolutionary.

But his death is the mustard seed that is destined to eventually take over the whole garden. Where can one find that mighty Roman Empire today? Only in the history books. It has been dead for 1,700 years. Yet now, on every single Sunday, no less than one billion people gather together all around the globe in every nation to confess that Jesus Christ is Lord of all and the world's true ruler. His empire truly stretches to the ends of the earth![5]

But here is where we need to park for a few moments and give time for serious reflection. The mustard seed of Christ's death reveals to us both the *nature* of God's work

[5] See Psalm 2:8.

in the world and also *how it spreads*. Calvary reveals to us that the nature of God's kingdom is one of love, forgiveness, humility, mercy, peace, and self-sacrifice. But contained within its very nature is also the means by which the kingdom expands.

Think of it this way. A mustard seed carries within itself the organic material required for its own growth and reproduction. One only needs to plant the seed, give it proper care, and then allow it to do naturally what it is meant to do. Its growth does not need to be controlled or engineered. All that is needed is cooperation.

In the same way, when communities of believers give themselves fully to imitating our Savior, this way of life naturally captivates people. Authentic Christianity intrinsically provides the essential ingredients for its own spread. Growth does not need to be driven by external strategies and techniques.

Just as the mustard seed is small and seemingly insignificant, *Jesus people* are those who have been formed in the way of humility, meekness, mercy, and peace-making. They are not seduced by the glamourous and the grandiose. Nor are they sucked into the undertow of an *us-versus-them* world. They have learned to be calm and content. They have learned to walk in wisdom and courage. See, this is not just *how* the kingdom spreads. It *is* the kingdom that spreads. This is what the world looks like under the reign of Christ. And it's the kind of Christianity that actually changes the world. Look no further than the testimony of the early Christian movement.

THE ORGANIC GROWTH OF EARLY CHRISTIANITY

While it is certainly not helpful to romanticize the early church, the fact remains that we have much to learn from our spiritual ancestors. During the first 270 years of church history, the Christian movement encountered various forms of persecution.

Throughout that period, a range of social and economic pressures were a constant factor in Christians' daily lives. While violent persecution was intermittent and rarely widespread, it was always an ever-present possibility. Because of these circumstances, there were no organized community outreaches or evangelistic events, as we think of them today. Christianity was outlawed and considered to be a dangerous cult. While evangelism was certainly happening, it was occurring on a personal and organic level.

In addition, throughout much of that time, many Christian communities would not even allow unbaptized people to participate in their official gatherings. Before one could even enter these assemblies, one had to go through a formational process that involved instruction and the practice of daily disciplines designed to thoroughly assimilate a candidate into the Christian way of life. This formational process would carry on for a period of up to three years (or more) and each candidate was assisted and observed by a "sponsor" throughout this span of time. Only after this process could one experience water baptism and join the official gatherings of a congregation.[6]

This practice may appear quite strange to modern Western Christians. But in an environment of persecution, it was necessary to be rather careful about admitting new people into these gatherings. Any unfamiliar person could be a potential informant against them.

But there was another crucial reason why the early church instituted this practice. In a culture of paganism and pervasive immorality, they believed that admitting

---

[6] For more information on this process, see *Resilient Faith* by Gerald Sittser (Ada, MI: Brazos Press, 2019) or *The Patient Ferment of the Early Church* by Alan Kreider (Ada, MI: Baker Academic, 2016).

new people too swiftly would effectively dilute the movement of the very essence that was attracting people in the first place. These early followers of Jesus placed a premium on faithfully preserving the distinctive character of the Christian way of life, trusting that the aroma of Christ upon their lives would naturally attract the pagan world around them. Alan Kreider, professor of church history and mission, writes: "Christians did not worry that absence of the pagans from their services constituted a lost opportunity. Their worship was not evangelistic; it was not 'seeker sensitive.' Their intent in worshiping was to glorify God rather than to attract outsiders. And since they believed that authentic worship formed the worshipers, they believed that in the course of time the behavior of those so formed would attract outsiders."[7]

According to early church historians, what attracted people to Christianity was the everyday lifestyle of its followers. As Christians embodied the Jesus way in how they cared for one another, looked after the poor and marginalized, and loved their enemies, their lives exhibited such a stark contrast to the world around them that people were drawn to their movement.

---

[7] Alan Kreider, *The Patient Ferment of the Early Church* (Ada, MI: Baker Academic, 2016), 189.

Sociologists estimate that during the first 270 years of church history, Christianity grew at an astounding rate of 40 percent per decade! This numerical growth was not engineered by aggressive outreach strategies nor slick marketing campaigns. It was the uncoordinated and unstoppable result of fully committed believers living out their faith in Jesus Christ. Early Christians were not concerned with triggering numerical growth through their own ingenuity. Their focus was on being faithfully formed in Christ and embodying his teachings. They considered numerical growth to be God's work, not their own.

Whenever Christianity is being faithfully practiced, it contains a beauty and allure that renders every church marketing tactic unnecessary and obsolete. However, when church communities are diluted by cultural compromise, even the slickest advertising campaigns and growth strategies will eventually fail. It may take a few months, a few years, or a few generations. But sooner or later, salt that has lost its saltiness will be exposed for what it is and discarded.

THE MENACE OF CONSUMERISM

I am convinced that one of the greatest challenges to the organic spread of authentic Christianity in modern America is the impulse to leverage the power of consumerism. In our society, if companies desire to grow bigger and faster, the prevailing question is, "What will appeal to consumers?" The greater appeal a product has, the more the customer base will expand, and the more quickly the company will grow. The all-important goal is swift, ever-increasing expansion achieved through the development of products that are designed to attract more customers.

Therefore, the ever-present temptation for churches in America is to adopt this philosophy of consumerism as a means for achieving organizational expansion. Indeed, many have done so unapologetically. In one of the largest megachurches in America, a poster was hung outside the pastor's office with the following questions: "What is our business? Who is our customer? What does the customer consider value?"[8]

---

[8] C. Christopher Smith and John Pattison, *Slow Church* (Downers Grove, IL: IVP Books, 2014), 40.

For many American churches, statistical growth is no longer seen as a natural result of genuine discipleship. Instead, it has become the governing principle by which leaders make decisions. It is seen as an achievable goal that can be reached through attractional techniques. And the easiest way to attract people into our churches is to identify what they want and give it to them. Once leaders adopt this mentality, the inevitable result is that they will begin to shape nearly everything they do based on how it will appeal to the consumers they are targeting. And it *works*. It can be an incredibly effective way to gather a following and expand a congregation.

However, a consumeristic approach to discipleship is simply not the way that people are formed in the self-sacrificial character of Christ, in which we become less and Jesus becomes more. Instead, consumeristic Christianity actually reinforces a self-centered, individualistic mindset, training people to ask questions like: *How is this church benefitting me? What more can this church offer me? Is this church meeting the needs of my family? Is this the best use of my time? Did I enjoy the song selection today? Did I feel inspired by the sermon this morning?*

When it comes to advancing the kingdom of Christ, consumerism is not our ally. Nor is it a neutral force we should harness. It is a serious enemy we must combat. It may help grow churches, but as long as statistical growth is our measuring stick for success, it is possible that we may achieve our goals and feel validated by our metrics, and yet totally fail at our mission of making disciples of the Jesus way.

Disciples cannot be mass produced. They are only handmade. Jesus is not a mass industrialist running a factory assembly line, churning out Christians. He is a patient artisan who handcrafts them one at a time. Page after page in the gospel narratives, he is the one who in the midst of a frenzied crowd is willing to stop in his tracks and give attention to a blind beggar, a grieving father, a suffering widow. Jesus didn't teach his disciples about assimilation systems and growth trends. He spoke to them about prodigals and lost sheep.

Whether a church is numerically large or small, church leaders must recognize that our primary task is to become and replicate authentic apprentices of Christ. And though we may create efficient systems with clear and identifiable "steps" for people to follow, discipleship is an inherently inefficient process. Because *people* are involved. And people are unique. And their lives are messy. Steering them into classes and growth tracks and calling it "discipleship" may keep the train rolling down the tracks, but the inconvenient truth is that it can actually hinder one's capacity for spiritual growth. Discipleship requires flexibility, patience, and personal care and attention. It cannot be mass produced through a one-size-fits-all system. Nor can it be measured on a graph. But the stories that emerge can and should be celebrated along the way.

The work of discipleship is also a long, laborious process. It doesn't always produce fruit right away. Our cultural blend of consumerism and technological advancement has created within us an expectation for instantaneous results. We are used to having everything we want immediately at our fingertips. Therefore, we tend to desire microwaved discipleship. God prefers a quality slow-roast.

Therefore, let us daily place ourselves in the heat of God's loving presence. Allow the pressures and anxieties of unrealistic expectations to melt away. And as local churches, let us follow the path of meekness and continue to gather together to worship, pray, share meals, teach, and serve our neighbors. Because Christ is building his church.

His church will outlive all of us. And the gates of hell shall not prevail against it.[9]

[9] See Matthew 16:18.

REFLECTION QUESTIONS
CHAPTER FOUR

1. What does *meekness* mean? How does the life of Jesus display meekness in perfected form? Recall some examples.
2. How does the way of meekness contrast with the American way?
3. What are some possible indicators that a person may be feeding off of their own religious performance or ministry output?
4. What are some ways leaders can keep their ambition in check?
5. What lessons regarding meekness do we learn from the parable of the mustard seed? How do these lessons apply to church life?
6. In what particular way is God calling you personally to walk the path of meekness?

CHAPTER FIVE

THE CRAVERS OF RIGHTEOUSNESS

Doing advocacy for good causes is urgent. But more urgent, in my view, is the nurture of venues of obedient imagination in which unuttered possibility is uttered, thoughts beyond our thoughts are thought, and ways beyond our ways are known.

—Walter Brueggemann, *Reality, Grief, Hope*

"Blessed are those who hunger and thirst for *righteousness*, for they will be filled" (Matthew 5:6). Few biblical words cause as much misunderstanding among churchgoers as the word "righteousness." In many Christian circles, righteousness is assumed to have something to do with the moral purity of one's heart and daily conduct. Therefore, the meaning of the fourth Beatitude is often understood in this way: "Blessed are those who want to live clean and pious lives, for they shall be spiritually satisfied." However, this interpretation causes us to miss the entire point.

The Greek word translated "righteousness" is *dikaiosune*. Interestingly, it also happens to be the Greek word translated "justice." In a broad sense, *dikaiosune* means "the state of things being right" or "things being as they should be."

In Hebrew, *righteousness* and *justice* are two separate words (*tsedaqah* and *mishpat*, respectively), however the terms are frequently connected in the Jewish prophetic tradition.[1] *Tsedaqah* (or "righteousness") has to do with *right relationship with God. Mishpat* (or "justice") has to do with *right treatment of neighbor*. They are, in fact, two sides of the same coin.

So for Jesus, a "righteous" person is someone who is in proper relationship with God (vertically) and also with others (horizontally). This is precisely his point when he is asked to identify the greatest commandment in Matthew 22: "'You shall love the Lord your God with all your heart, and with all your soul, and with all your mind.' This is the greatest and first commandment. And a second is like it: 'You shall love your neighbor as yourself.' On these two commandments hang all the law and the prophets" (Matthew 22:37-40).

In the fourth Beatitude, Jesus' use of the term *dikaiosune* combines these two concepts into one. Indeed, the teaching of the New Testament considers them to be inseparable.[2] In other words, right worship of God is

---

[1] See Isaiah 5:7 and Amos 5:24 for examples.
[2] See Matthew 7:12, John 13:4, Galatians 5:14, 1 John 4:20-21, and 1 Peter 3:8 for a few examples.

inextricably linked to right treatment of others. Our love for God is meant to be intimately connected with our love for neighbors (enemies included[3]).

HOLY DISRUPTION

The importance of this connection can be observed in the ministry of the prophet Jeremiah. Roughly six hundred years prior to the birth of Christ, Jeremiah was known as a preaching poet who became God's prophetic voice, speaking to the nation of Judah. During his era, the rich and powerful upper crust of Jerusalem would gather regularly at the temple to worship God with prayers and sacrifices. But they were also notorious for profiting from injustice. They were neglecting the poor and exploiting their workers. After loaning money to poor farmers at outrageous interest rates, they would foreclose on them when the debtors were unable to pay back the loan. The rich lenders would then seize the property. The wealthy elite were lining their pockets by abusing the weak and vulnerable without pity.

---

[3] See Matthew 5:43-48 and Luke 10:25-37.

During this same period, Babylon was emerging as a formidable power. Located north and east of the land of Judah, it presented an imposing threat to the Jewish capitol. But the powerful and privileged of Jerusalem were unconcerned. They were convinced that nothing disastrous could ever happen to them, because after all, they had God on their side. They considered their beautiful temple to be God's own dwelling place on earth. Who could ever cause harm to them and their magnificent city? As long as they continued offering the proper rituals of prayer and sacrifice, they deemed themselves to be safe and untouchable.

And yet, once they concluded their worship gatherings, they would leave the temple and continue their abusive mistreatment of the least of society. They would ruthlessly take advantage of the indigent, the widow, and the foreigner. So one day Jeremiah stands at the entrance of the temple, and as people attempt to pass through the gates, Jeremiah begins to cry out:

> This is what the Lord Almighty, the God of Israel, says: Reform your ways and your actions, and I will let you live in this place. Do not trust in deceptive words and

say, "This is the temple of the Lord, the temple of the Lord, the temple of the Lord!"

If you really change your ways and your actions and deal with each other justly, if you do not oppress the foreigner, the fatherless or the widow and do not shed innocent blood in this place, and if you do not follow other gods to your own harm, then I will let you live in this place, in the land I gave your ancestors for ever and ever.

Will you steal and murder, commit adultery and perjury, burn incense to Baal and follow other gods you have not known, and then come and stand before me in this house, which bears my Name, and say, "We are safe"—safe to do all these detestable things? Has this house, which bears my Name, become a den of robbers to you? (Jeremiah 7:3-7; 9-11a).

The privileged elite were viewing the temple as a safehouse for oppressors. They assumed that as long as they worshiped God in the temple, they would be protected from the consequences of their exploitation. So Jeremiah tearfully disrupts their worship to give them a graphic warning that disaster is coming: "The carcasses of this people will become food for the birds and the wild animals, and there will be no one to frighten them away. I will bring an end to the sounds of joy and gladness and to the voices of bride and bridegroom in the towns of Judah and the streets of Jerusalem, for the land will become desolate" (Jeremiah 7:33-34). And alas, this is exactly what happened. In 587 BCE Nebuchadnezzar's army besieged Jerusalem, massacred its inhabitants, torched the temple, and leveled the city to the ground. All survivors were taken and deported to Babylon. It was an earth-shaking moment that continues to reverberate across history to this very day.

Six hundred years after Jeremiah's warning, another Jewish prophet would stand at the entrance to the Temple Mount. Just like their ancient counterparts, the wealthy and influential temple elite had again been using their positional authority to exploit the common people for their own personal gain. And what Jesus would do next would be the most provocative prophetic act of his entire life—one that would actually seal his fate: "Then he entered the temple and began to drive out those who were selling things there; and he said, 'It is written, "My house shall be a house of prayer; but you have made it a den of robbers''''' (Luke 19:45-46).[4]

By driving out the money changers, Jesus momentarily shuts down the function of the temple during the busy season of Passover. Then quoting from the words of Jeremiah, he re-enacts Jeremiah's warning with the message that impending disaster is once again coming upon Jerusalem. This connection is made explicit in the preceding verses: "Indeed, the days will come upon you, when your enemies will set up ramparts around you and surround you, and hem you in on every side. They will crush you to the ground, you and your children within you, and they will not leave within you one stone upon another; because you did not recognize the time of your visitation from God" (Luke 19:43-44).

Just as in the days of Jeremiah, the temple had become a haven for thieves. The chief religious officials had turned it into a machine of corruption for personal profit. They assumed that as long as they preserved the ritualistic practices of worship unto God through their prayers and sacrifices that God would shield them from the consequences of their injustice. And Jesus declares that

---

[4] See also Isaiah 56:7 and Jeremiah 7:9.

they are gravely mistaken and warns them of devastating consequences ahead. *They will not leave within you one stone upon another.*[5] Only one generation later in 70 CE, the Romans would ravage Jerusalem, burn the temple to the ground, and brutally slaughter tens of thousands of people.

Like Jeremiah, Jesus was not seduced or intimidated by the influential power owned by the temple leaders. Nor was he moved by the sheer size of their system of worship. The meaning of his prophetic act in the temple courts is unmistakable. Jesus refuses to put his stamp of approval upon acts of worship that are not coupled with right treatment of others. It does not matter how earnest our intentions may be. Right worship is always linked with right treatment of people. Any system of worship that is content to ignore the cries of the broken and oppressed is completely out of touch with the heart of Christ and his gospel message.

THE FULL SCOPE OF THE GOSPEL

The "good news" of the Christian gospel is not simply that Jesus has come to save souls so that we can go to heaven

---

[5] See Matthew 24:2.

when we die. Yes, Jesus saves souls (he is in the process of saving mine). And yes, between our own death and resurrection we are absent from the body and present with the Lord in heaven.[6] So I affirm these truths.

But this is not the primary essence of the gospel message heralded by the apostles. The gospel is the announcement that the world now has a new supreme ruler, Jesus Christ, who has won an atoning victory through his cross and resurrection. The apostle Paul speaks of salvation as something that happens even now as we are transferred into the kingdom of God's beloved Son.[7] In other words, right here and right now, we are to be living in allegiance to the world's true redeemer, working together to carry out his heavenly agenda on earth.

Through Jesus, God has reconciled all things in heaven and earth.[8] The problems that presently exist in the world are pervasive and overwhelming. But God has no plans to leave the world in ruins. God is saving and redeeming it. God is setting everything *right*. And as ambassadors for Christ we are invited to become participants even now in God's reclamation project. This is what we acknowledge

---

[6] See 2 Corinthians 5:8.
[7] See Colossians 1:13.
[8] See Colossians 1:13-20.

when we pray, “Your kingdom come. Your will be done, on earth as it is in heaven” (Matthew 6:10).

Therefore, Christians aren’t simply to sit around waiting for the afterlife. We are to align ourselves with God’s reconciling work throughout all of creation and human society under the reign of Christ. This is the gospel proclaimed consistently by the prophets and apostles. It also happens to be the message of this verse from one of the most beloved carols we sing every Christmas season:

> He rules the world with truth and grace, and makes the nations prove
>
> The glories of his righteousness, and wonders of his love[9].

“And makes the nations prove…” In Matthew 25, Jesus gives us a glimpse of himself seated upon his heavenly throne judging the nations. He casts a vision of people separated into two groups. To the first group (the sheep) he gives a wonderful inheritance:

---

[9] Isaac Watts. Lyrics to “Joy to the World.” *Timeless Truths*, 2020, library.timelesstruths.org/music/Joy_to_the_World/

> Then the king will say to those at his right hand, "Come, you that are blessed by my Father, inherit the kingdom prepared for you from the foundation of the world; for I was hungry and you gave me food, I was thirsty and you gave me something to drink, I was a stranger and you welcomed me, I was naked and you gave me clothing, I was sick and you took care of me, I was in prison and you visited me… Truly I tell you, just as you did it to one of the least of these who are members of my family, you did it to me" (Matthew 25:34-35; 40).

However, here is how he addresses the second group (the goats):

> Then he will say to those at his left hand, "You that are accursed, depart from me into the eternal fire prepared for the devil and his angels; for I was hungry and you gave me no food, I was thirsty and you gave me nothing to drink, I was a stranger and you did not welcome me, naked and you did not give me clothing, sick and in prison and you did not visit me.' Then they also will answer, 'Lord, when was it that we saw you hungry or thirsty or a stranger or naked or sick or in prison, and did not take care of you?' Then he will answer them,

> 'Truly I tell you, just as you did not do it to one of the least of these, you did not do it to me.' And these will go away into eternal punishment, but the righteous into eternal life" (Matthew 25:41-46).

This passage introduces several notable topics, but the most significant point has to do with the basis for this separation. According to Jesus, the determining factor separating the sheep and the goats has nothing to do with a verbal confession of faith. Rather, it hangs upon our treatment of the hungry, the thirsty, the stranger, the naked, the sick, and the prisoner. In fact, this matter is of such importance to Jesus that he even personally identifies himself with these oft-neglected groups. "Truly I tell you, just as you did it to one of the least of these who are members of my family, you did it to me."

Now Christians may have varying opinions on how to best care for prisoners, immigrants, the poor, and the sick. But what is undeniable is that our just treatment of the least of these is of top concern to our heavenly king. And as his ambassadors, we pledge allegiance to him and are devoted to his agenda. Right?

THE ACHE FOR JUSTICE

One of the great champions for justice in American history is Frederick Douglass. Douglass was truly an American prophet in the mold of Jeremiah. Born into slavery in 1817, he eventually escaped two decades later and settled in Massachusetts, where he became known as a preacher, writer, and abolitionist.

During this era of American history, the institution of slavery was causing enormous division not only throughout society but even within Christian churches. Many American pastors were either shamefully supporting slavery or excusing it as an unfortunate but necessary evil in an economy dependent upon cheap farm labor.

But Douglass had a hunger in his heart to see justice for the oppressed. In 1845, eighteen years before the Emancipation Proclamation, he penned these words:

> Between the Christianity of this land and the Christianity of Christ I recognize the widest possible difference… I hate the corrupt, slave-holding, women-whipping, cradle-plundering, partial and hypocritical Christianity of this land… We have men-stealers for

ministers, women-whippers for missionaries, and cradle-plunderers for church members...

The man who wields the blood-clotted cowskin during the week fills the pulpit on Sunday, and claims to be a minister of the meek and lowly Jesus. The man who robs me of my earnings at the end of each week meets me as a class-leader on Sunday morning, to show me the way of life, and the path of salvation. He who sells my sister, for purposes of prostitution, stands forth as the pious advocate of purity. He who proclaims it a religious duty to read the Bible denies me the right of learning to read the name of the God who made me...

The slave auctioneer's bell and the church-going bell chime in with each other, and the bitter cries of the heart-broken slave are drowned in the religious shouts of his pious master. Revivals of religion and revivals in the slave-trade go hand in hand together. The slave prison and the church stand near each other... The dealer gives his blood-stained gold to support the pulpit, and the pulpit, in return, covers his infernal business with the garb of Christianity. Here we have religion and robbery the allies of each other."[10]

These are the prophetic words of a man who embodied the fourth Beatitude. To "hunger and thirst for righteousness" is to share in the burden of God over the brokenness of the world and to be willing to do something about it.

For two thousand years, such yearning has led Christians to establish hospitals, relief organizations, orphanages, public education, and charities for the poor and hungry. Those who are being formed in the character of Christ refuse to cooperate with corrupt systems (whether natural or human-created) that deface the image of God in others.

GLOBAL POVERTY

The brokenness of the world can be observed in a multitude of issues: human trafficking, child labor, systemic racism, disease, substance abuse, pollution,

---

[10] Frederick Douglass, *Narrative of the Life of Frederick Douglass, an American Slave* (Boston: Anti-Slavery Office, 1845).

abortion, genocide, totalitarianism, and human violence (to name only a few). But rather than attempting to explore all of these issues, let's zoom in on one particular issue: global poverty. According to the World Bank,[11] 736 million people currently live in extreme poverty, defined as living on less than $1.90 per day. Half of these are children. Three-quarters of these children live in Asia and Sub-Saharan Africa. [12] In Sub-Saharan Africa, one out of every three children will experience stunted growth because of malnutrition. This stunted growth affects cognitive ability, making it more difficult for them to succeed in the classroom. For malnourished children who survive, the average child suffers up to 160 days of illness each year. [13] Approximately 3.1 million children die every year from diseases directly related to malnutrition.[14] This amounts to 8,493 children dying of malnutrition *every single day*. Innocent children. The most vulnerable among us.

---

[11] "Poverty and Equity Data Portal," The World Bank, http://povertydata.worldbank.org/poverty/home/ Apr. 26, 2020.
[12] World Hunger Education Service (WHES), "World Child Hunger Facts," Hunger Notes, https://www.worldhunger.org/world-child-hunger-facts/, *Worldhunger.org*. Apr. 26, 2020.
[13] WHES, "World Child Hunger Facts."
[14] WHES, "World Child Hunger Facts."

Meanwhile, the nations of the world spend $4.98 billion *per day* on their defense programs—36 percent of that spending by the United States (China comes in second place with 13 percent).[15] So in other words, for every single child who dies of hunger, the nations of the world spend $586,365 on their programs to defend themselves from one another.

I do realize that military spending is a hot button issue. But I am only giving facts. At the very least, followers of Jesus Christ should all be able to look at statistics like these and say, "There is something terribly wrong with the world. Surely, this is not how God desires things to be. And I ache for things to be made right."

A VISION FOR RIGHTEOUSNESS

Too often, the response of local churches to the problems of the world is something like this: "Let's put aside the problems of injustice and just focus on spreading *the gospel* and getting people *saved*." But this response reflects a

---

[15] Aaron Mehta. "Here's How Much Global Military Spending Rose in 2018." Defense News. Apr. 28,2019. http://www.defensenews.com/global/2019/04/28/heres-how-much-global-military-spending-rose-in-2018/,. Apr. 26, 2020.

counterfeit gospel that is powerless before the powers and principalities that keep human society bound by evil. *Conversion* certainly has its place, but what, after all, are people being converted to?

Abolitionists such as William Wilberforce didn't seek to end slavery in England by simply converting all of the slave owners. They worked with one another to establish new laws that changed the configuration of their society, thereby eliminating the demonic institution of slavery. Any version of Christianity that ignores the pervasive problems of the world is a toothless Christianity that presents very little threat to the kingdom of darkness.

Yes, evil is widespread in the world, and the problems that result can seem insurmountable. But those who are shaped by the fourth Beatitude refuse to bow in allegiance to the status quo. They dare to imagine and contend for a world of *shalom* under the reign of King Jesus, because this world indeed belongs to God, and God intends to redeem it from its bondage.

The local church is ground zero for this work of redemption. Our communities of faith should be places where disciples gather to worship Jesus passionately. But we should also remember that he is the same Jesus who was willing to disrupt worship to expose systems of oppression and injustice. If our acts of worship form us to be people who care for the least and the marginalized, then our worship is holy before God. But proper worship should always lead us to care for the weak, the vulnerable, and the oppressed. Worship and justice go hand-in-hand.

This connection is fostered first within our own faith communities and then flows outward to the larger society. Local churches are called to embody God's vision for the world under the reign of Christ. The wider culture should be able to observe our faith communities and say, "Here is a place where relationships are genuine, where people are made whole, where self-sacrificial love is supreme, and where the poor are properly cared for. This is what the entire world should be like." In this sense, the local church actually becomes a visual example of life in God's new creation.

No single church will ever correct every wrong that exists in the world (or even within its own city). We are finite human beings who are incapable of saving the world by ourselves. But we can each share a portion of God's pain and work to expand the kingdom within our own sphere of influence. Church leaders aren't meant to create a program for every problem. Sometimes our role is to simply identify willing servants who have a unique burden and connect them to existing needs.

But it all begins with being willing to share God's ache over the brokenness of human society. As apprentices of Jesus, may we refuse to shrug our shoulders in passive resignation at the presence of evil. May we allow ourselves to feel God's pain over the world and begin to pray, "Thy kingdom come, thy will be done on earth as it is in heaven." And may that pain disrupt our selfish patterns of living and inspire us to work together for creative solutions. May we dare to believe that the church of Jesus Christ can actually make disciples of the nations.

REFLECTION QUESTIONS
CHAPTER FIVE

1. What are some common misunderstandings of the word "righteousness," and how do they cause us to miss Jesus' point in this Beatitude?
2. What connections exist between Jeremiah's prophetic message in Jeremiah 7 and Jesus' symbolic shutdown of the temple six hundred years later? Why is it important to understand this connection?
3. If God will ultimately set everything right, why should Christians care about justice in the world today? Why is justice a gospel issue?
4. Can you identify examples of men and women who have lived with a hunger and thirst for justice?
5. What are some current problems that exist in your locale that create a hunger in your heart for justice?
6. In our efforts to work for justice, how can we establish boundaries and limits to keep ourselves spiritually healthy?

CHAPTER SIX

THE MERCIFUL

The line separating good and evil passes not through states, nor between classes, nor between political parties either—but right through every human heart—and through all human hearts. This line shifts. Inside us, it oscillates with the years. And even within hearts overwhelmed by evil, one small bridgehead of good is retained.

—Aleksandr Solzhenitsyn, *The Gulag Archipelago*

Billy Sunday is widely considered to be the most influential American revivalist of the early twentieth century. A former Major League Baseball outfielder, Sunday eventually converted to Christianity and became a traveling minister, using his athletic fame to promote tent crusades across the United States. It is estimated that throughout his evangelistic career, Sunday preached over 20,000 sermons to more than 100 million people.

It was Sunday who popularized the phrase "sawdust trail." In order to keep the dust down and to dull the noise of shuffling feet, crusade organizers would line the aisles of these makeshift assemblies with sawdust. To *hit the sawdust trail* was to walk down the aisle at the conclusion of the sermon and shake Sunday's hand as a public demonstration of one's decision to become a Christian. Sunday used to say that the best thing that could happen to a person would be to attend one of his revival meetings and get "saved," then walk out into the road, get hit by a Mack truck, and die and go to heaven.

Perhaps he was being a bit facetious. Nevertheless, Sunday's comment reveals something about the emphasis of his message (which seems to be representative of a large segment of American evangelicalism). According to this particular brand of Christianity, Jesus is mainly a vehicle by which one gets to heaven.

When I was a young teenager, I participated in an evangelism course offered by my local church. We would gather weekly on Tuesday nights for training, and then we would split into groups and do house-to-house visitation in our community for the purpose of sharing our faith. For these home visits, we were given a ready-made script to follow consisting of several points accompanied with Bible verses. After beginning each conversation with pleasantries, we were to proceed with the following question: *If you were to die tonight, do you know if you would go to heaven?*

Now, I don't mean to minimize the value of this question. But for the Christian, there is another related question to consider. What if death *doesn't* come tonight? What if the Mack truck swerves to the other side of the road? There is still, after all, quite a bit of living to do. Afterlife issues aside, *how then shall we live?*

When the chief focus of our evangelistic proclamation is about *getting to heaven*, we are (perhaps unwittingly) perpetuating a distorted understanding of the Christian life. Over the course of modern history, this is exactly what has happened within evangelical Christianity, and we must wrestle with its cause and effects.

The Sermon on the Mount has nothing to do with how to get to heaven when you die. It's all about how to live the human life right here and right now. Jesus is giving us a vision of the new, proper, redeemed way to be human. And at the center of this vision is mercy.

CHANNELS OF MERCY

Throughout Jesus' famous sermon, *mercy* is a consistent theme. We are taught to pursue reconciliation with those who have offended us, to turn the other cheek, to love our enemies, to refrain from condemning others, and to treat others how we want to be treated.[1] And in the middle of the sermon, Jesus teaches us to pray: "And forgive us our debts, as we forgive our debtors" (Matthew 6:12 NKJV).

Mercy is part of the very essence of the Christian experience. A Christian is one who has first received mercy from God—not merely in the form of a legal transaction, but by being reconciled to God in relationship. And within that relationship, one continues to experience the outpouring of mercy on a daily basis. As this is happening, one becomes trained and empowered to practice mercy towards others.

This transformational process finds its basis in Christ's crucifixion. The cross is not only where we come to find mercy. The cross is where we also find our model for living. Jesus didn't say, "I'm taking up my cross so that you don't have to." He said, "Take up your cross and follow me."[2] Meaning, *do it like I do it*. On the cross Jesus perfectly embodies his message. In turn, we are now called to become cross-shaped people towards one another.

So Christians believe in the forgiveness of sins. Yes, we believe in experiencing God's forgiveness. But we also believe in extending forgiveness towards those who sin

---

[1] See Matthew 5:23, 5:29, 5:44, 7:1, 7:12.
[2] See Matthew 16:24.

against us. In a wounded world that is dominated by the instinct for vengeance, local churches are to be channels through which the healing mercy of God flows. Without such mercy there is really no hope for the world.

More than anyone else in history, Jesus had both the right and the means to retaliate against his enemies. But instead he extended his arms upon the cross and prayed, "Father, forgive them" (Luke 23:34). On the cross, Jesus showed *the way* by absorbing humanity's hatred, violence, and evil and putting them to death through his response of divine love and mercy. Thus, by his wounds an injured world can now find the path of healing and salvation for which it so desperately yearns.

As we become shaped by his mercy and carry forth this message of forgiveness throughout the world, we become agents of healing. When we absorb the wrongs of others and follow Christ in offering mercy, we help loose the chains of demonic hatred and retaliatory violence that keep the world bound in evil.

RECIPROCAL MERCY

The fifth Beatitude is commonly translated this way: "Blessed are the merciful, for they will receive mercy"

(Matthew 5:7). It is an inverted rendering of the famous line of the Lord's Prayer: "And forgive us our debts, as we also have forgiven our debtors" (Matthew 6:12). In other words, mercy is received by those who are willing to give it to others. This is a point Jesus makes explicitly in this middle of the Sermon on the Mount: "For if you forgive others their trespasses, your heavenly Father will also forgive you; but if you do not forgive others, neither will your Father forgive your trespasses" (Matthew 6:14-15). However, some scholars point out that according to the syntax of the Beatitude, the Greek conjunction *hoti* (translated "for") can also be properly translated "seeing that." According to this view, the statement would then be rendered this way: "Blessed are the merciful, *seeing that* they will receive mercy." This version of the statement would indicate that the *reception* of mercy is actually what empowers one to *show* mercy to others in the first place.

Regardless of which translation is correct, both lead to the same conclusion. *Mercy is reciprocal.* Mercy is a river that is constantly flowing. Once it meets a barrier, it simply changes course to find another channel that will cooperate with its flow.

I have used a morning prayer liturgy every day for several years.[3] It includes silence, scripture, and my own spontaneous prayers. But I also include an assortment of structured prayers that have been formed by the community of faith and used for hundreds of years. Near the end of my prayer time, I typically include a wonderful prayer of thanksgiving found in Thomas Cramner's *Book of Common Prayer*. In the middle of the prayer, there is a beautiful line: "And, we pray, *give us such an awareness of your mercies*, that with truly thankful hearts we may show forth your praise, not only with our lips, but in our lives…"[4]

Whether we realize it or not, each of us is actually swimming in the mercy of God. Every breath I take into my lungs is, indeed, a merciful gift from God. Every beat of my heart is an expression of God's unbounded love towards me. The issue isn't whether we are recipients of God's mercy. Our existence depends upon it. The issue is

---

[3] This prayer liturgy was assembled by Brian Zahnd, pastor of Word of Life Church in St. Joseph, Missouri. I highly recommend his weekend "prayer school" events offered periodically throughout the year.

[4] Episcopal Church, "Daily Evening Prayer: Rite Two," *The Book of Common Prayer* (New York: Seabury Press, 1979), 125, my emphasis.

how much awareness we may have of God's mercy at any given moment.

When we are slow to recognize and appreciate God's goodness to us, we are then slow to open our own hearts to one another. The sin of unforgiveness can only fester in the heart of a person who remains completely out of touch with his or her own desperate need for God's boundless mercy. On the other hand, as we become more aware of God's limitless love endlessly cascading into our lives, the more we are then empowered to forgive even our worst enemies. And the nexus point that makes all of this possible is Calvary.

Within evangelical Christianity we rightly view Christ as our mediator who stands between us and God. Yet, Christ also intends to mediate our own relationships with one another, and indeed with the world itself. Bonhoeffer wrote: "Since Christ, there has been no more unmediated relationship for the human person, neither to God nor to the world."[5]

For the Christian, there can be no unmediated relationships. Christ stands between me and anyone I may encounter on a given day. Therefore, God's vision for my

---

[5] Dietrich Bonhoeffer, *Discipleship* (Minneapolis: Fortress Press, 2003), 94.

life is that I perceive every person I meet through the lens of Calvary. No matter who that person is nor what choices that person has made, I am seeing a person who contains unsurpassable worth. How do I know that? Because Jesus paid an unsurpassable price on that person's behalf. So as I grow in the practice of loving my enemies and forgiving my transgressors, I am partaking in the divine nature and reflecting the beauty of Calvary. This is what intimacy with God looks like at its highest peak.

Jesus absorbed the blow of human sin on the cross and responded with radical forgiveness. Hence, following Jesus will entail a willingness to absorb the wrongs of others without retaliation. In this manner, showing mercy necessitates a readiness to *embrace* suffering. Now, this is not a popular message. And it is certainly not the American way. But it is the Jesus way. And it *is* the power of the gospel that can actually transform the world.

Showing mercy doesn't mean we ignore the wrongs of others or forget about them. Indeed, justice and mercy are meant to go hand-in-hand.[6] But the act of mercy involves releasing those wrongs to God and trusting that God will ultimately set everything right. In the meantime, we

---

[6] See Micah 6:8.

choose to walk the path of forgiveness and end the cycle of vengeance. In this way, we are walking the path of Calvary, honoring our Savior.

PRACTICING MERCY

Mercy is truly a practice of self-denial. When another person or group has wounded me, my natural reaction is to harbor ill-will against them and to possibly even strike back in anger and bitterness. And the more I rehearse the offense internally, the more entrenched those negative emotions become. Therefore, it is crucial that we understand that the practice of mercy is not something each of us can do on our own. Walking the way of mercy requires the continual infilling of God's Spirit.

One of the disciplines that I have found to be immensely helpful in this regard is a daily exercise of reflective prayer. To illustrate, let's suppose one of my neighbors is attempting to destroy my reputation by making untrue comments about me to others around my neighborhood. When I learn of this, I feel both angry and discouraged. These initial feelings are completely unavoidable and entirely justifiable. The question, though, is *how will I respond?*

It would be one thing for me to simply express my rage to God in prayer. This can actually be a healthy practice. If I cannot bring my honest emotions before God, where else should I bring them? Above all else, God invites us to be authentic in prayer, to bring our whole selves to God, including our emotions and thought patterns. Indeed, many of the psalms are quite shocking in their expressions of rage and resentment towards enemies. If we do not bring our anger before God in prayer, we are denying God access to an essential part of what makes each of us human.

However, it will not do for me to merely express my anger towards my neighbor to God in prayer and then walk away. Instead, I have also learned in moments like these to sit still and to be quiet for a certain length of time. I remind myself that I am in the presence of a loving God. I gratefully reflect upon the truth that I am an undeserving recipient of God's extravagant mercy. And as I sit in silence, I have now relinquished control of the prayer to God.

It is in this environment that I am now able to submit this troublesome situation to the agenda of heaven. My fractured ego has now been subsumed into God's loving presence, and I am now primed to see this situation from a different perspective. Perhaps God may allow me to see that this neighbor of mine has been severely hurt by others and is responding out of the pain of a wounded soul. In fact, God might even enable me to identify and acknowledge my own past attitudes and actions towards my neighbor that have contributed to this woundedness. Regardless, the point is not to excuse my neighbor's actions nor to assign blame to myself (warranted or unwarranted). The point is to be still and give God an opportunity to show me a broader perspective, so I can respond to this person in the posture of Calvary-formed mercy.

This prayer exercise is definitely not easy, fun, or painless, but it helps form me in the way of Calvary. And the more often I engage in this practice, the more it will begin to reshape my patterns of thought and behavior until mercy becomes engrained into my very way of life.

This practice of mercy applies not only on a personal level, but also to the divisions and hostilities that characterize our wider society. We live in a contentious culture in which people tend to immediately demonize one another over varying political opinions on virtually any conceivable issue. America truly is a mercy-starved society. And where else will she find mercy than from among those who have been thoroughly formed by the fifth Beatitude?

Being merciful doesn't always mean changing your conclusion. Nor does it mean withholding your opinion. It simply involves seeking to understand first, and then giving the other person or group the space to hold an opposing view without demonizing them. Just like anyone else, Christians have a right to contend in the public marketplace for the ideas and values we believe contribute to a healthy society. But if in the midst of our political efforts we neglect to walk in mercy, we have stumbled off the narrow path and have conformed to the patterns of hostility found within the broader culture.

GROWING IN MERCY TOGETHER

The primary setting in which we learn to walk in mercy is within our local churches. As we regularly gather together with the same group of men, women, and children to worship, pray, break bread, learn, share stories, and spend time together, life itself will present us with countless opportunities to sharpen one another in the virtues of the Christian faith.

One of the early church fathers, Tertullian, is credited with stating, "One Christian is no Christian." In order to properly mature in Christlikeness, each of us must be deeply rooted within a local church family. Yes, sometimes being committed to one particular church over a long period of time can result in a certain degree of pain. But there is simply no other way to cultivate mature Christian character. Any supposed version of the Christian faith that is not embodied within an actual church family will eventually be exposed as weak and ineffectual. We must have relationships with other believers that are close enough to produce conflict, which provides us with opportunities to grow in the practice of mercy.

This commitment to authentic community is another way in which radical Christianity is a revolt against consumerism. A consumeristic mentality says, "*Find an appealing church that is catered to my interests and filled with people who are just like me and who happen to share the exact same opinions that I have.*" Once you find a promising church, you begin to attend and get involved. But over time, you eventually realize that the church isn't quite measuring up to your expectations. So the search begins anew every few months or years. This is not to say that there aren't valid reasons for someone to occasionally choose a different church. But ideally, these situations are rare. New Testament scholar Joseph Hellerman writes: "We have been socialized to believe that our own dreams, goals, and personal fulfillment take precedence over the well-being of any group—our church or our family, for example—to which we belong. The immediate needs of the individual are more important than the long-term health of the group. So, we leave and withdraw, rather than stay and grow up, when the going gets rough in the church or in the home."[7]

In a society that values individuality, independence, and the personal pursuit of happiness, Christians are unequivocally called to give ourselves to Christ and to one another. Imagine someone who might say, "I was so disappointed with my Christmas experience last year with my family. The roast was overcooked. The tree wasn't decorated to my liking. And there was a bit too much conversation about politics and not enough talk about sports. This year I'm going to have Christmas with the family next door." This would obviously be ludicrous. And yet, it is similar to how many American churchgoers approach their relationship with their own local congregations.

Throughout the New Testament, one of the most

---

[7] Joseph Hellerman, *When the Church was a Family: Recapturing Jesus' Vision for Authentic Christianity* (Nashville: B&H Publishing Group, 2009), 4.

common metaphors used to describe the local church is that of a *family*.[8] For those who confess Christ as Lord, the local church is not a competitive enterprise that exists to peddle products in order to appeal to consumers and increase its market share. A local church is a family to which you belong. Healthy families learn to love and extend mercy to one another in the midst of irritations and disagree-ments.

This is Christ's vision for his church. Many of the New Testament instructions such as "love one another," "[forgive] one another," and "be at peace with one another"[9] presuppose that conflict and tensions will arise within our relationships. From Jesus' perspective, conflict is not a barrier to authentic Christian discipleship. It can actually be an ideal catalyst for transformation.

Therefore, each of us have much to gain from rooting ourselves in a local church with people *who are most unlike ourselves*. If I have my own way, I tend to gravitate to people who are just like me. I naturally congregate with people who share common interests with me, who have a similar

---

[8] For a few examples, see Matthew 12:49-50, Romans 12:10, Galatians 6:10, Ephesians 2:19, 1 Timothy 3:15, and 1 Timothy 5:1-2.

[9] See John 13:34, Ephesians 4:32, and Mark 9:50.

background, and who see the world the same way as I do. But when I am rooted in a local church it forces me to mingle with all kinds of people.

When I get to choose who I spend time with and how often I spend time with them, it's relatively easy for me to get along with people. But when I plant myself within a local church family filled with people of all kinds of backgrounds, personalities, life stages, and viewpoints, there will be some serious opportunity for real discipleship. Joe Beach writes: "We have to share life together close enough and long enough to truly hurt and offend one another enough to require real forgiveness. We have to spend enough quality time with each other to truly experience enough annoying, irritating differences to make acceptance genuinely meaningful."[10]

To the degree that I isolate myself from anyone who may potentially cause me offense, I am short-circuiting my own potential for spiritual growth. The local church is the garden where Christians grow. Make no mistake, it requires serious work and dedication. But if I have any hope of growing in mercy, it will happen in connection

---

[10] Joe Beach, *Ordinary Church* (St. Joseph, MO: Spello Press, 2019), 62.

with such a church, a mercy-formed community that illuminates a dark world.[11]

[11] See Matthew 5:14-16.

REFLECTION QUESTIONS
CHAPTER SIX

1. If you have some sort of religious background, what do you remember about the way you were taught regarding the meaning of Jesus' death on the cross?
2. What do you think it means for us to become cross-shaped people?
3. In John 3:17, Jesus declares that he came not to condemn the world (*kosmos*), but that the world through him might be saved. What do you think it means that the world can be saved through Jesus?
4. How can one go about cultivating a life of mercy?
5. How does the practice of mercy require one to embrace the path of self-denial?
6. In what ways can local churches be the ideal place for one to become formed in the practice giving mercy? How have you seen this happen?

CHAPTER SEVEN
THE PURE-HEARTED

Holy people, however much they may enjoy being themselves, are not obsessively interested in themselves. They allow you to see not them, but the world around them. They allow you to see not them, but God. You come away from them feeling not, "O, what a wonderful person," but "What a wonderful world," "What a wonderful God," or even, with surprise, "What a wonderful person I am too."

—Rowan Williams, *Being Disciples*

"Blessed are the pure in heart, for they will see God" (Matthew 5:8). Essential to orthodox Christian faith is the confession of the divinity of Christ. Jesus of Nazareth was not merely a religious guru, a prophet, an enlightened teacher, or an ideal moral example to follow. The consistent claim of the New Testament is that he is the unique, eternal, and divine Son of God. Jesus explicitly stated, "Whoever has seen me has seen the Father."[1] The author of Hebrews tells us that Jesus is no less than "the

---

[1] See John 14:9.

exact imprint of God's very being."[2] Paul explains that Christ is "the image of the invisible God."[3]

Our English word *incarnation* comes from the combination of two Latin words: *in* (meaning "in") and *carnis* ("flesh"). It is from the Latin word *carnis* that we get the modern Spanish word *carne* ("meat" or "flesh"). So if I sit down at a Mexican restaurant and order *chili con carne*, I am ordering "chili with meat." Jesus is God *con carne*. God *in the flesh*. God *incarnate*.

From the very beginning, as Jesus launched his ministry and began traveling throughout the region of Galilee, people immediately began to marvel at the unusual work of God that was happening through this mysterious man. Not quite sure what to make of Jesus, the crowds were always speculating about his possible identity and role within the scope of Israel's prophetic destiny. But by and large, the multitudes were certain that whoever this man happened to be, the hand of God was surely upon him.

But not everyone was able to *see* God at work in Christ. There was a particular religious party in first-century Israel known as the Pharisees. The Pharisees were a sizable faction who promoted moral and religious purity within

---

[2] See Hebrews 1:3.
[3] See Colossians 1:15.

the Jewish world. They believed that this state of purity would somehow be the impetus for God to deliver Israel from enemy occupation and restore its sovereign identity. In all of Israel, the Pharisees were held in the highest regard for their unparalleled commitment to honoring God. But oddly enough, when *God incarnate* showed up in their midst, they fiercely opposed him. Here is a particularly memorable example: "Then they brought to [Jesus] a demoniac who was blind and mute; and he cured him, so that the one who had been mute could speak and see. All the crowds were amazed and said, 'Can this be the Son of David?' But when the Pharisees heard it, they said, 'It is only by Beelzebul, the ruler of the demons, that this fellow casts out the demons'" (Matthew 12:22-24).

Consider the irony here. They literally demonized Jesus, revealing their spiritual blindness. And it happened in response to Jesus curing an actual demoniac of physical blindness. How could this group that was so regarded for their religious devotion not only fail to see the work of God through the divine Son, but *accuse* him of being in league with the *Accuser*?

What kept the Pharisees spiritually blind was not sin, per se. Because, after all, everyone who encountered Jesus was a sinner in some fashion. In fact, many of those who were considered to be among the worst of sinners in Israel were the first to rejoice upon his arrival and receive the good news of the kingdom. What blinded these religious experts from seeing God at work in Jesus was a particular *category* of sin. The sins of externalism: hypocrisy, judgmentalism, and religious pride.

THE CIRCUS GORILLA

In the early 1930s, during the height of the Great Depression, a Louisiana cotton farmer was in grave danger of losing his farm. He was desperately searching for some way to supplement his income in order to save his livelihood.

One weekend, a traveling circus stopped in his town. As soon as he could, he scheduled a meeting with the circus manager to ask him for a job. He told the man, "I'll do anything you need. I just need some extra money."

The circus manager didn't even hesitate. "Not only is the job yours, but I'm going to turn you into a huge star. And you're going to earn more money than you've ever made in your life."

This response made the farmer a bit nervous. "Wait a moment. You just met me for the first time only a few seconds ago, and now you're going to hire me on the spot and pay me all of this money? What kind of job are we talking about here?"

The manager replied, "Well, here's the situation. Our gorilla, Coco, had been our biggest attraction for several years. People loved Coco. He was the most important part of our entire show. But unfortunately, Coco died last week. And in these tough economic times, we certainly cannot afford to import another gorilla from overseas. So instead, we've created a gorilla suit, and we would like for you to wear it and take Coco's place, performing the gorilla act in our circus."

Of course, this conservative Louisiana farmer had no desire to ever become a circus gorilla. But he also didn't want to lose his farm. So he swallowed his pride, put on the gorilla suit, and joined the circus.

Every night a rope hung from the peak of the big top out over the lion's cage. At the climax of the show, the "gorilla" was to grab the rope and swing over the lion's cage several times while throwing bananas at the lion. The rope was carefully measured so that no matter how high the lion leapt, it could not reach the gorilla. And the crowds absolutely loved it. It was their favorite part of the show. Every night they would give the gorilla a standing ovation.

Surprisingly, after the first couple of nights the farmer realized he was beginning to enjoy his new job. After all, he had never received a standing ovation after plowing rows on his farm. So he embraced his new role with great gusto, learning how to imitate all of the sounds and mannerisms one might expect from a gorilla.

One night he decided to take things up a notch. When it came time for him to begin his act, he grabbed the rope with one hand and began to swing over the lion's cage. In his other hand, he was clutching a rolled-up newspaper. When the lion leaped into the air, he leaned back and used the newspaper to swipe the lion straight across the jaw. But just as he connected with the lion's jaw, he forgot about his other hand which was holding the rope!

Instantly, he tumbled to the floor of the cage. The lion immediately pounced on him and began to roar in his face. At this moment, he completely forgot that he was supposed to be imitating a gorilla, and he began to scream at the top of his lungs, "Someone help me! Get me out of here! Please! I'm going to die!"

Then the lion leaned forward and whispered in his ear, *"Shut up, you fool! You're going to get us both fired!"*

RELIGIOUS EXTERNALISM

One may look like a gorilla, sound like a gorilla, smell like a gorilla, and behave like a gorilla, but all the while be a man zipped up in a monkey-suit. The ever-present danger for anyone who begins the journey of faith is the potential to embody a sort of *monkey-suit Christianity*, in which one bears all of the external markers of Christian commitment but neglects to pay attention to the deeper issues of the soul. Once this begins to happen, one has ventured off the path of Calvary and onto the broad road of religious pride and hypocrisy.

This shift into externalism is nearly imperceptible to the person involved, but it is truly toxic to one's spiritual health. While everything may look exactly as it should on the exterior of one's life, there is a lethal virus latent beneath the surface. And once it takes root, it can be quite difficult for the person to even recognize its presence.

Jesus had a habit of exposing the externalism that existed in the lives of many of the Jewish leaders of his day. Each of his stinging rebukes were his loving attempts to awaken them to their blind condition:

> "Woe to you, scribes and Pharisees, hypocrites! For you clean the outside of the cup and of the plate, but inside they are full of greed and self-indulgence. You blind Pharisee! First clean the inside of the cup, so that the outside also may become clean.
>
> Woe to you, scribes and Pharisees, hypocrites! For you are like whitewashed tombs, which on the outside look beautiful, but inside they are full of the bones of the dead and of all kinds of filth. So you also on the outside look righteous to others, but inside you are full of hypocrisy and lawlessness" (Matthew 23:25-28).

Jesus comments on externalism within the Sermon on the Mount. In one segment, he refers to those "hypocrites" who draw attention to their practices of prayer, fasting, and generous giving so other people will praise them.[4] Elsewhere, Jesus again uses the word "hypocrites" to describe religious leaders who elevate religious traditions over the supreme responsibility of loving others.[5] He then quotes from Isaiah: "These people honor me with their lips, but their hearts are far from me" (Matthew 18:5 NIV).

---

[4] See Matthew 6:1-18.
[5] See Matthew 15:7.

His frequent clashes with these leaders over their objections to his acts of healing on the Sabbath repeatedly expose this deadly virus of religious hypocrisy. Jesus teaches that the entire sum of the Law and the Prophets boils down to the commands to love God and our neighbors.[6] And yet, these religious leaders use their own adherence to religious standards to elevate themselves at the expense of others.

It is important to recognize that this condition of spiritual blindness is not something that God has inflicted upon them. To the contrary, Jesus (who perfectly embodies God's will on earth) keeps pleading with them in hopes of that they will eventually be set free from their condition of blindness.

SPIRITUAL SIGHT

For a moment, imagine your inner life as having a window. Windows accomplish two things. First, a window allows light from the outside to enter a room. This would have been especially important in the ancient world before the age of electricity. Without any windows, a person would

---

[6] See Matthew 22:37-40.

live in relative darkness. But secondly, a window also allows someone in the room to look through it to see outside of the house. Thus, a window allows us to see both inside and outside.

But if the window is never cleaned, and grime is allowed to accumulate to the point that it eventually becomes caked over with filth, it will no longer serve any useful function. One will live in darkness and will be unable to see through to the outside. What we learn from Jesus' interaction with these religious experts is that the grime that accumulates on the window of the soul is not just any particular sin. It is the joint sins of hypocrisy, judgmentalism, and religious pride that keep us in spiritual blindness.

One of these confrontations occurs after an amazing miracle of Jesus healing a man who was blind from birth. In that culture, it was commonly assumed that one who is blind must be bearing God's judgment for some grievous sin. When some of the Pharisees learn of this man's healing, they attempt to discredit Jesus and even call him as a sinner.[7] In response, Jesus declares, "I came into this world for judgment so that those who do not see may see,

---

[7] See John 9:24.

and those who do see may become blind."[8] This entire incident illustrates Jesus' point. The man who was born blind now has new sight, both physically and spiritually.[9] Yet, the Pharisees who claim to have pristine spiritual perception, cannot identify the very Son of God who stands right in front of them.

Once the virus of religious hypocrisy takes root in one's heart, it has the potential to thoroughly destroy that person's ability to perceive and cooperate with the work of God on earth. What makes this virus particularly insidious is that as it grows within one's inner life, everything may look exactly right on the outside. Yet all along, the incongruence between the interior and exterior life only continues to worsen.

SEEING GOD AT WORK

A number of years ago our church launched a long-term residential program for men with addictions. It has since become an incredibly fruitful endeavor that God has blessed in so many astonishing ways. Once a man enters our program, we provide him with food and lodging for

---

[8] See John 9:39.
[9] See John 9:38.

an entire year, equip him through life-on-life discipleship, and train him in vocational skills with the goal of placing him in a suitable job and living arrangement upon graduation.

Early in our program, one of the young men (I'll call him "George") participated in the filming of an informational video on behalf of the ministry. Sitting in front of a beautiful cross, George briefly shared part of his story. For several years, his life had been controlled by an addiction that resulted in the loss of his job, estrangement from his family, and ultimately confinement in a jail cell. Out of desperation, he finally made a decision to seek help. He landed with us, and after spending a year in the program, the trajectory of his life began to dramatically change.

In the video George could hardly contain his excitement as he described the restoration that was happening in his family and in his own personal life. He had a huge smile beaming across his face as he expressed gratitude for God's mercy upon his life. The video closed with George expressing his desire for God to use him to help and serve others who have come from similar backgrounds. The video was filmed, edited, and later shared on social media. Immediately, it began to go viral. Tons of people commented that they were thrilled to hear about the change in this young man and the healing that was occurring within his family.

The joy and celebration were *nearly* unanimous. But alas, a certain individual had an objection. This person had been known in the local community for being a self-styled theological "watchdog." He had built quite a reputation for consistently barking at other Christians, preachers, and churches who didn't happen to agree with his view on seemingly any issue. (Of course, the trouble with watchdogs is they often can't tell the difference between a thief and a mailman.)

Upon watching the brief two-minute video, this man happened to notice what he felt was an apparent flaw in George's theology. It occurred to him that as George shared about the change in his life, he neglected to use specific terms like "repentance," "blood of Jesus," or "born again." Therefore, though he had never met George or had a single conversation with him, he found it appropriate to publicly cast suspicion upon George's walk with Christ by making a post on social media.

Now, the actual intent of the video was simply to promote the program. It wasn't meant to serve as a proper testimony of George's Christian conversion. The men in our ministry have other opportunities to give a more thorough testimony, most notably at their baptism. But this video was filmed as a tool to spread awareness about the program to other individuals and families suffering through addiction.

To this day, George continues to walk in freedom from the addiction that kept his life bound for so many years. He is still young in Christ, but the glory of God continues to shine through his life. George may not be as theologically articulate as some, but the work of God in his life has been amazing to witness.

There is so much more gospel hope found in stories like George's than can ever be found in the smug judgmentalism of those who are able to define terms like "atonement" and "propitiation" but cannot see the work of God happening right in front of their very eyes.

Over the years, I have been grieved to witness friends and acquaintances who, for whatever reason, latch onto unhealthy and toxic preaching that propagates a similar form of religious externalism. While all of the external markers may be present, the fruit that is produced bears no resemblance to the life exemplified by Jesus hanging on the cross praying for his executioners. At the end of the Sermon on the Mount, Jesus warns us: "Beware of false prophets, who come to you in sheep's clothing but inwardly are ravenous wolves. You will know them by their fruits. Are grapes gathered from thorns, or figs from thistles? In the same way, every good tree bears good fruit, but the bad tree bears bad fruit" (Matthew 7:15-17).

Here, Jesus is drawing upon a common motif from the pen of Isaiah, who loved to use fruit-related imagery in his prophetic declarations. And according to Isaiah, the fruits that God longs for are righteousness and justice.[10] In other words, we are called to live in right relationship with God and with one another. This is exactly the subject matter of the entire Sermon on the Mount encapsulated by the Beatitudes. Therefore, according to Jesus' warning, there is a certain kind of "false prophet" whose ministry actually works *against* the value system set forth in the Beatitudes. These ravenous wolves (Jesus' term, not mine) mercilessly ignore the cries of the meek and the oppressed, and all the while seek to gain power and influence by consistently demonizing other leaders (whether religious, political, or otherwise). And their distinguishing characteristic is religious pride.

---

[10] For my favorite example, see Isaiah 5:1-7.

Jesus warns us to beware of those whose lives display a veneer of religiosity, but do not produce the fruits of righteousness and justice. If we constantly feed on influences that are contaminated with self-righteousness and legalistic pride, the virus of religious arrogance will take root in our hearts and even begin spreading amongst the people around us. Perhaps it may be helpful to take a few moments and personally reflect on the following questions:

- Who are the primary influences in my life (authors, preachers, leaders, podcasters, etc.)?
- Do they inspire me to crave more for God's presence (and not just beat me down if I don't)?
- Are they capable of seeing God at work in other churches, ministries, and leaders (or have they confined God to their own rigid box)?
- Do they empower me to live a contented life with Christ (or do they inject anxiety and insecurity into my spiritual life)?
- Do they encourage me to follow the Calvary way of living humbly, walking in mercy, and loving my enemies?

- Do they motivate me to live a more others-oriented life?

In the interest of spiritual health, we must intentionally surround ourselves with humble-hearted, life-giving people who are genuinely fascinated with Jesus, the true Bread of Life, and share his burden to reconcile all things and all people to the Father.

The sixth Beatitude teaches us that our capacity to see God is connected with the purity of our own hearts. If the windows of our hearts are clean, then we will be able to perceive the work of God in others. But if our hearts have become polluted with pride and hypocrisy, then all we will notice are their sins and faults.

It requires no keen spiritual perception to look at other people and point out their deficiencies. To use Jesus' term, any *blind fool* can do that. Spiritual sight is the ability to look at other people, other places, and other churches and identify the handiwork of God. As our hearts become purged of spiritual pride, we will begin to see everything with fresh eyes. And all of creation will become a beautiful, panoramic vision of the glory of God.

REFLECTION QUESTIONS
CHAPTER SEVEN

1. What are some possible reasons that many of the religious leaders of Jesus' day were not able to see God at work in his ministry?
2. Why do you think Jesus uses such strong language in his rebukes of these leaders?
3. Recall some examples from the gospel accounts of people who had enough purity of heart to see God's hand at work in Jesus. What types of things do these people have in common?
4. Why are the sins of externalism (hypocrisy, pride, judgmentalism) so seductive and dangerous? What are some of the indicators that these sins are taking root in one's heart?
5. What are some practices we can adopt with other believers in order to keep our hearts pure from religious pride?
6. Where can you presently identify God at work in your church family? In your community? In your relationships with family and friends? In the lives of your enemies?

CHAPTER EIGHT
THE PEACEMAKERS

Rather than using his power to distance himself from us, Jesus uses it to approach us. He follows his own commandment to love your neighbor as yourself—often to his detriment, I might add—by pursuing *us* with great tenacity in spite of our differences.

—Christena Cleveland, *Disunity in Christ*

Shalom. It is the Hebrew term at the root of the biblical vision for "peace." But the concept of *shalom* is far richer and deeper than our common notions of *peace*. From a Judeo-Christian perspective, peace is not simply about the absence of commotion and conflict. *Shalom* is not defined merely by what is *absent*, but by what is *present*. It describes the beauty and harmony of a world exactly as God would have it to be.

In the beginning, all of creation was fashioned with the intention that each individual part would be fully integrated in unbroken unity, reflecting the splendor and majesty of the triune God. Just as the Father, Son, and Spirit dwell together in perfect, self-giving love, God's dream was that the entire cosmos would reflect and mutually participate in this beautiful, harmonious relationship. *Shalom*.

For this purpose, God created human beings, empowering them with the authority to rule over certain fundamental aspects of creation.[1] Because the very essence of God is love, and love does not coerce or control, God gave these beings genuine freedom. On the basis of love, God's desire was that these created beings would freely choose to bring everything under their authority into alignment with God's rule.[2]

Unfortunately, instead of using their authority to help integrate the world under God's agenda, they rebelled against God, causing *dis*integration.[3] Therefore, as a result of human and angelic rebellion, nothing currently functions according to its original design. Even creation itself has become subject to decay and destruction. Rather

---

[1] See Genesis 1:26-31.

[2] Greg Boyd has written an insightful essay regarding the role of Satan and other cosmic forces in the corruption of nature (https://reknew.org/2019/07/satan-and-the-corruption-of-nature-seven-arguments/).

[3] See Romans 8:20.

than reflecting the *shalom* of God, it has become a cosmic war zone.[4]

Thankfully, God did not abandon us in this condition. God's divine Son became a human being who has won an atoning victory on the cross in order to bring an end to this cosmic struggle. Through his self-sacrificial death, Jesus ultimately has defeated the powers and principalities which have kept creation bound, and has become the means by which all things are once again being reconciled in perfect *shalom* with the triune God.[5]

This victory has already been established in principle. *Shalom* has already been accomplished through Christ's victory on the cross. But we obviously don't yet see its full manifestation throughout creation and human society. This is what theologians have referred to as the "already but not yet" paradox of God's kingdom. Yes, Jesus has *already* defeated his enemies and is now ruling as Lord of all. But this reality is *not yet* completely demonstrated throughout the cosmos. When Christ ultimately returns, his victory will finally permeate every square-inch of

---

[4] For more on this cosmic warfare, see Gregory Boyd's book, *God at War: The Bible and Spiritual Conflict* (Downers Grove, IL: IVP Academic, 1997).
[5] See Colossians 1:20.

creation. Until then, we continue to live in the crossfires of a spiritual war.[6]

It is from within this context that we can now begin to understand the seventh Beatitude. When Jesus calls us to be *peacemakers*, he means something other than "conflict-avoiders." He means that we are to first reflect and carry within us the kind of integrated wholeness and harmony reflected within God's own self. And then we are to participate together in the Spirit-led work of ushering human society and creation itself into this new world of *shalom*.

Blessed are the peacemakers, for they will be called children of God (Matthew 5:9). This work of peacemaking is not passive. Nor is it for the faint of heart. Scot McKnight defines peacemaking as "an active entrance into the middle of warring parties for the purpose of creating reconciliation and peace."[7] But as we work together to manifest *shalom* in our relationships and throughout creation, we are bearing a family resemblance to the "God of peace."[8]

---

[6] See Ephesians 6:12.
[7] Scot McKnight, *The Sermon on the Mount Commentary* (Grand Rapids, MI: Zondervan, 2013), 47.
[8] See Romans 16:20.

THE INSTRUMENT OF PEACE

The Romans frequently used the term *Pax Romana*, meaning "the peace of Rome." Beginning with the reign of Caesar Augustus, Rome experienced an era of relative peace and stability throughout the empire that lasted for roughly two centuries. But it was peace that came through terror and domination. The empire spread "peace on earth" by the point of a sword. As the Romans continued to conquer and subjugate surrounding nations, they preserved the peace by brutally crushing any hint of rebellion.

Their favorite device of terror was the Roman cross. Crucifixion was designed to prolong death and to make it as torturous as possible. The Romans crucified tens of thousands of people, sometimes even subjecting entire towns to mass execution at once. They would commonly perform these crucifixions alongside of major roads and intersections, leaving the victims to hang for days as a public reminder of the price of rebellion. Therefore, ironically the Romans brought peace to the world through the cross.

But within hours of his own arrest and crucifixion, Jesus would tell his apostles, "My peace I give to you. I do not give to you as the world gives" (John 14:27). The Roman Empire brought peace by taking their enemies and nailing them to crosses. Jesus would take that same instrument of torture and transform it into an instrument of *shalom*. As Paul writes to the Colossians: "and through [Jesus] God was pleased to reconcile to himself all things, whether on earth or in heaven, by making peace through the blood of his cross" (Colossians 1:20).

Like Caesar, Jesus uses the cross as an instrument to establish peace, but he does so in a profoundly different fashion. Rather than exacting vengeance upon his enemies and nailing *them* to crosses, he absorbs their hatred and violence by humbly giving himself up on the cross. Instead of calling upon legions of angels to avenge his blood, he chooses to pray, "Father, forgive them."

This is the ultimate act and example of peacemaking. In the midst of a world that is hopelessly hellbent on hostility, Jesus relinquishes his own heavenly tranquility and deliberately steps into the conflict, recycling vengeance into reconciliation. By doing so he provides the foundation for a new world of *shalom*—the dream of the Hebrew prophets.

> Rejoice greatly, O daughter Zion!
> Shout aloud, O daughter Jerusalem!
> Lo, your king comes to you; triumphant and victorious is he, humble and riding on a donkey, on a colt, the foal of a donkey.
> He will cut off the chariot from Ephraim and the war-horse from Jerusalem; and the battle bow shall be cut off, and he shall command peace to the nations; his dominion shall be from sea to sea, and from the River to the ends of the earth (Zechariah 9:9-10).

Jesus Christ came not simply to bring an inner, emotional peace within the hearts of individuals. He came to establish *shalom* upon the earth—a kingdom of peaceful harmony that transcends national and ethnic barriers. In his letter to the Ephesians, Paul addresses the intractable conflict in the early church between the Jewish believers and the Gentile converts by re-founding their identity around the cross: "For he is our peace; in his flesh he has made both groups into one and has broken down the dividing wall, that is, the hostility between us. He has abolished the law with its commandments and ordinances, that he might create in himself one new humanity in place of the two, thus making peace, and might reconcile both groups to God in one body through the cross, thus putting to death that hostility through it" (Ephesians 2:14-16).

Christ is the cosmic peacemaker. Because we are incorporated into Christ, we share in his nature, and therefore, are destined to display his peacemaking character in the world. And to the degree that *shalom* characterizes our lives and relationships, we are resembling our *Abba* in heaven.

CHRIST THE DISRUPTOR

The point is often made that peacemaking is not synonymous with peacekeeping. But to take it even further, sometimes *keeping* peace can actually be the polar opposite of *making* peace. Peacemaking often demands the courage to disrupt the status quo.

As soon as Jesus launches his public ministry, news begins to spread rapidly throughout the region of Galilee about this formidable teacher and miracle-worker. It is during this time that Jesus preaches his first recorded sermon in his hometown of Nazareth. The ancient Jewish village of Nazareth was located just a few miles from the border with the region of Syro-Phoenicia. For many centuries, the various Gentile groups that occupied this vast territory were considered to be among Israel's most despised enemies. The hatred that simmered between them frequently spilled into violence and bloodshed. (Indeed, this animosity continues between the modern nation-states of Israel and Syria to this day).

So Jesus shows up one Sabbath in the synagogue of Nazareth, the synagogue where Jesus would have gathered with his family every Sabbath throughout his entire childhood. As he stands to take his place, he is surrounded by friends and family who have known him for many years. They are well-aware of his rising fame and are quite proud to call him one of their own.

As Jesus begins to teach, he opens a scroll and begins to read from a famous messianic passage recorded by the prophet Isaiah.[9] He then sits down and announces, "Today, this scripture is fulfilled in your hearing." With these words, he is unequivocally associating himself with the messianic figure of Isaiah's prophecy. So far, so good. The people of Nazareth are enthused by what they are hearing. Luke tells us, "All spoke well of him and were amazed at the gracious words that came from his mouth."

---

[9] See Luke 4:16-30 (Jesus quotes from Isaiah 61:1-2a).

But then the sermon takes a bizarre turn. Jesus begins to describe the contours of his messianic kingdom by connecting it with two highly controversial stories found in the Hebrew scriptures. First, he references an episode involving the prophet Elijah. Jesus explicitly points out that though there were many widows throughout Israel who suffered mightily during the lengthy famine of Elijah's day, God went out of his way to miraculously provide for a Syro-Phoenician widow from Zarephath.

The second story Jesus mentions is even more provocative. He remarks on the story of Naaman the leper—not only a hated Syrian but the commander of the Syrian army (which happened to be in a vicious war with Israel at the time)! And yet again, Jesus reminds his Jewish audience that there were many lepers living in Israel during those days. And yet, God did not send the prophet Elisha to heal any of them. He healed only Naaman the Syrian.

By bringing up these two stories, Jesus is turning their messianic expectations upside-down. He gives them a flavor of what his kingdom will be like. Rather than catering to those who considered themselves to be insiders, Jesus declares his intention to swing the doors wide open for anyone and everyone, including their own worst enemies. Through his sermon he essentially informs them, "Yes, I am the Messiah. But I refuse to endorse your cherished hostilities against your Gentile neighbors." And immediately, the crowd erupts in anger and attempts to hurl him off a cliff.

This is the risk of true peacemaking. When one refuses to participate in the game of *us versus them*, and instead dares to confront the source of hostility itself, resistance will typically come from multiple directions. Therefore, peacemaking is dangerous work. But it is *gospel* work. Those whose chief aim is to perpetually avoid conflict will often find themselves standing in opposition to God's dream for *shalom*.

LETTER FROM A BIRMINGHAM JAIL

On Good Friday, April 12, 1963, Dr. Martin Luther King, Jr. was arrested and detained in Birmingham, Alabama. King was jailed for his participation in organizing several nonviolent protests that a circuit court judge had previously ruled illegal.

On the day of King's arrest, eight white clergymen in Birmingham published a public statement through the local newspaper. They voiced their relative support for the cause of civil rights and acknowledged that the organized protests were peaceful and nonviolent. However, they discouraged further demonstrations, warning that they would only incite hatred and violence, and thereby undermine the cause of racial justice in Birmingham.

In the interest of keeping the peace, they suggested that King and his fellow activists should pursue justice through the courts rather than demonstrating in the streets of Birmingham. The letter stated: "We recognize the natural impatience of people who feel that their hopes are slow in being realized. But we are convinced that these demonstrations are unwise and untimely."[10]

The missive provoked King to respond with a letter of his own, written from his jail cell. In King's masterful response, he effectively defended his involvement on biblical grounds and patiently explained that the approach these ministers were calling for had already been attempted numerous times without success. The civic institutions of Birmingham were plagued with systemic injustice, preventing any semblance of progress toward

---

[10] A Group of Clergymen, "Letter to Martin Luther King," April 12, 1963, TeachingAmericanHistory.org, https://teachingamericanhistory.org/library/document/letter-to-martin-luther-king/

justice and leaving these civil rights workers with no other recourse.

As King explained, there had been "more unsolved bombings of Negro homes and churches in Birmingham than in any other city in the nation."[11] In fact, only five months later the Sixteenth Street Baptist Church in Birmingham would be bombed, claiming the lives of four precious little girls. This was not the season to sit cautiously on the sidelines and hope for the best. Making peace required a more direct and active approach. To his fellow clergymen, King pointedly remarks:

> I have almost reached the regrettable conclusion that the Negro's great stumbling block in his stride toward freedom is not the White Citizen's Counciler or the Ku Klux Klanner, but the white moderate, who is more devoted to "order" than to justice; who prefers a negative peace which is the absence of tension to a positive peace which is the presence of justice…

---

[11] Martin Luther King, Jr., "Letter from a Birmingham Jail," April 16, 1963, Africa.upenn.edu, https://www.africa.upenn.edu/Articles_Gen/Letter_Birmingham.html

> I had hoped that the white moderate would understand that the present tension in the South is a necessary phase of the transition from an obnoxious negative peace, in which the Negro passively accepted his unjust plight, to a substantive and positive peace, in which all men will respect the dignity and worth of human personality.[12]

To be a peacemaker frequently requires the courage to step into the fire and confront the evils that keep humanity bound. Like King, it will often result in enduring some measure of persecution. But this is precisely the Calvary trail that Jesus blazed two thousand years ago. The peacemaker is one who is willing to relinquish personal comfort and be placed in harm's way for the sake of *shalom* on earth.

PEACEMAKING WITHIN THE CHRISTIAN COMMUNITY

For the Christian, the focal point for the work of peacemaking is first within actual congregations of believers. It is much easier for us to dream about and pray

---

[12] King, "Letter from a Birmingham Jail."

for peaceful reconciliation in the midst of some geopolitical conflict occurring elsewhere in the world than it is for us to directly address the hostilities within our own assemblies.

Much of the content of the New Testament epistles has to do with making peace between believers who are worshiping together. Throughout these ancient letters, we find instructions for making peace—between the wealthy and the poor, between Jewish believers and Gentile converts, between family members dwelling under the same roof, and between those who held different theological opinions on "disputable matters."[13] In each of these scenarios, the focus is on actual relationships occurring within local congregations.

We will only be able to establish *shalom* throughout the earth to the degree that *shalom* is present within the body of Christ, first within its local assemblies. This peace does not happen to us by accident or through osmosis. We must contend for it. Because we live in a "me first" culture, the work of peacemaking necessitates that we be prayerfully formed in the practices of humility and self-denial. Jim Forest writes: "Sometimes Christ's peace seems especially

[13] See Romans 14.

absent among his followers. We don't simply disagree with one another on many topics, but we often despise those who hold what we regard as false or heretical views. Disagreement may be necessary—the defense of truth is a virtue—but hatred is a grave sin. Most often it isn't truth we battle for but opinion, vindication of our irritation with someone else, or just the desire to have things our own way."[14]

Within local churches, tensions and disagreements will inevitably happen. But this is no impediment to the mission God has given us. In fact, the fruit of peaceful unity can be cultivated only in the soil of conflict. Our willingness to contend for unity, even in the midst of sharp disagreement, forms part of our essential witness to the world. On the night of his arrest, Jesus prayed for the unity of his disciples: "I ask not only on behalf of these, but also on behalf of those who will believe in me through their word, that they may all be one. As you, Father, are in me and I am in you, may they also be in us, so that the world may believe that you have sent me" (John 27:20-21).

Local churches—drawn from people of different classes, ethnicities, and backgrounds—are called to assemble

---

[14] Jim Forest, *The Ladder of the Beatitudes* (Maryknoll, NY: Orbis Books, 1999), 126.

together under the reign of Christ and become viable communities of unity and peace. The apostle Paul explains that through these types of communities, "the wisdom of God in its rich variety [is] made known to the rulers and authorities in the heavenly places."[15] In other words, in a society that is intensely divided along ethnic, national, and political lines, when apprentices of Christ transcend these barriers and embody peace together under his reign, that unity establishes the credibility of our testimony to the world.

What holds us all together is our allegiance to Jesus. Within the body of Christ, we may hold contrasting opinions on all kinds of theological, political, and social issues. But our fidelity to Christ outweighs everything else. Of course, this doesn't mean that we should just suppress our differences by refusing to have difficult conversations regarding important issues. But if we facilitate division and enmity within our local churches, we then empower our spiritual enemy to impugn the credibility of our testimony to the wider society.

Therefore, we should engage in hard conversations over our differences. And even when agreement is not possible

---

[15] See Ephesians 3:6-10.

(and it won't always be so), we should instead choose to unite under the authority of Christ and live as one. This is how the world will come to know that Jesus truly is Lord of all. Paul writes to the Philippian church: "Do all things without murmuring and arguing, so that you may be blameless and innocent, children of God without blemish in the midst of a crooked and perverse generation, in which you shine like stars in the world" (Philippians 2:14-15).

The family of God is where we find our core identity. Our most fundamental bond does not come from a shared nationality, ethnicity, political platform, or familial relationship. We are, first and foremost, brothers and sisters in Christ. And this relationship surpasses every other bond or distinction. When we are able to hold our differences in mutual respect and strive to preserve our unity in Christ, we not only display profound spiritual maturity, but we proclaim the gospel through these very relationships.

Jesus famously instructed his disciples: "Salt is good; but if salt has lost its saltiness, how can you season it? Have salt in yourselves, and be at peace with one another" (Mark 9:50). The *saltiness* that creates *thirst* in the world for God's kingdom is the peaceable community of Christ's followers who have chosen to reject the way of hostility, and have instead given themselves completely to the vision of Christ.

THE WITNESS OF PEACEMAKING

In his frequent confrontations with the various Jewish powers and authorities, Jesus exposes their participation in four categories of injustice: oppression of the weak, exploitation of the poor, exclusion of the marginalized, and violence against their enemies. He understands that if they continue to travel down the wide road of greed, power-hunger, and violence, disaster will inevitably strike.

Just days before his arrest, Jesus stands on the Mount of Olives overlooking Jerusalem, the "city of peace." He begins to weep over the city, saying, "If you, *even you*, had only recognized on this day *the things that make for peace*!" (Luke 19:42) The peace he refers to is not simply an emotional peace within the hearts of individuals. This becomes clear as he continues: "Indeed, the days will come upon you, when your enemies will set up ramparts around you and surround you, and hem you in on every side. They will crush you to the ground…" (Luke 19:43-44). And of course, only one generation later, tensions erupt into a violent war between the Jews and the Romans that ultimately results in the siege and destruction of Jerusalem.

From the beginning of human history, the world has been hopelessly entrenched in a vicious cycle of hatred and revenge. But in the kingdom of Christ, Jesus calls us to follow him into the ways of peace. United under his Lordship, he summons us to care for the weak, and to swim against the cultural currents that pull us into hatred and violence against our enemies. "Love your enemies and pray for those who persecute you, so that you may be children of your Father in heaven; for he makes his sun rise on the evil and on the good, and sends rain on the righteous and on the unrighteous" (Matthew 5:44-45).

These words are no less radical today than they were on the day Jesus spoke them. He does not qualify his instruction. Whether our enemies are local, global, personal, or political, we are called to love them indiscriminately. And when people mistreat us, we are to pray for them. This is how we "overcome evil with good."[16] When we do so, Jesus says we resemble our Father in heaven, faithfully bearing God's image. This is the heavenly vision that local churches are called to embrace

---

[16] See Romans 12:21.

and embody, because this is what God is like. It is our unique Christian witness in a world at war.

This radical gospel of God's peaceable kingdom is the world's only hope. But it will become clear only as followers of Christ embody and proclaim the ways of peace. Jesus blesses the peacemakers. They are the ones who carry within them the identifying mark of the children of God.

REFLECTION QUESTIONS
CHAPTER EIGHT

1. In what ways does the biblical concept of *shalom* differ from modern notions of peace? Why is this significant?
2. How can Jesus' work on the cross be considered the ultimate act of peacemaking? How does Calvary provide us with a pattern for making peace with others?
3. What is the difference between peacemaking and peacekeeping?
4. Can you think of examples of modern peacemakers who have been willing to step into conflict for the sake of the common good?
5. Why should local congregations be considered "ground zero" for the work of peacemaking?
6. How does unity differ from uniformity? Why is unity something we must contend for?

CHAPTER NINE
THE PERSECUTED

Let wrongdoing grow weary from your patience.

—Tertullian, *De Patientia*

Mohammed Saeed Omer converted to Christianity while studying in college in New Delhi, India. Born in Sudan, Omer was raised by a devout Muslim family. When his parents learned of his conversion, they immediately demanded that he return to Sudan. After arriving home, Omer's parents seized his passport and began their relentless attempts to coerce him into renouncing his commitment to Christianity, even to the point of threatening to disown him.

When Omer remained steadfast in his devotion to Christ, his parents reported him to the General Intelligence Service of Sudan. Omer was ultimately arrested by the authorities who proceeded to torture him, extracting his fingernails with pliers. He was eventually delivered back to his parents where he was placed under constant surveillance. Three years later, with the aid of his local Christian community, Omer was finally able to escape Sudan and begin a new life in another country.

Many Western Christians are unaware of the nature and extent of persecution against our brothers and sisters all around the world. The source of this persecution is often governmental authorities, as it is in Burma, China, Iran, North Korea, Saudi Arabia, and Vietnam. In other cases, persecution comes from extremist groups that operate beyond government control. This oppression can take many forms—economic pressure, detention, imprisonment, forced labor, enslavement, rape, torture, and murder among them.

But regardless of its exact nature, persecution against Christians around the globe is massive in scale and serves as a sobering reminder to us that our loyalty to Christ must trump all other allegiances. Western Christians have much to learn from our brothers and sisters who faithfully persevere in the face of constant intimidation and threat of violence. We must continually pray for them, share their stories, and advocate on their behalf.[1] As we do so, we solidify ourselves with them in a manner that actually nurtures our own faith.

---

[1] For an enlightening perspective on global persecution including suggestions for ways to advocate for the persecuted Church, see *Persecuted* by Paul Marshall, Lela Gilbert, and Nina Shea (Nashville: Thomas Nelson, 2013).

SUFFERING FOR RIGHTEOUSNESS' SAKE

In his final Beatitude, Jesus announces, "Blessed are those who are persecuted for *righteousness'* sake, for theirs is the kingdom of heaven" (Matthew 5:10). Notice that Jesus specifically identifies those who are suffering "for righteousness' sake." We dealt with the concept of righteousness earlier when we examined the fourth Beatitude.

Righteousness, once again, has to do with the interrelationship of our worship of God with our just and loving treatment of one another. This combination of pure worship and shalom-making justice is possible only for those who are being shaped by the Beatitudes. Each Beatitude is deeply interconnected with the other seven. We cannot make peace if we are unwilling to mourn what is broken. We cannot show mercy if we have no capacity for meekness. We cannot absorb the blow of unjust persecution without humble hearts. Therefore, the eight Beatitudes are woven together, presenting a tapestry of life under the reign of Christ.

So the Beatitudes lead us into a deeper imitation of Christ. And in turn, this will entail embracing opportunities to bear the weight of suffering and opposition. George O. Wood writes, "The person who integrates into his or her life the principles of Christ's own life, embodied in the Beatitudes, becomes an individual whose goodness awakens the hostility of the world."[2]

As Jesus gives us the Beatitudes and fully embodies them in his life and teachings, his fate is sealed. The existing power structures of his day will not tolerate such a strange, radical movement that threatens the security of their social position. Likewise, when communities of faith have been properly formed by the Beatitudes, their very existence serves as a potent critique against the prevailing cultural forces of greed, lust, and abuse of power. Consequently, opposition of some kind is inevitable. This is a necessary part of what we experience when we imitate Jesus.

But taking this path of patient suffering is anything but a weak, spineless admission of defeat. It is our courageous participation in the counter-cultural revolution called the kingdom of Christ. Brian Zahnd writes: "Following the Jesus way of loving enemies and doing good to those who hate us isn't necessarily safe and it doesn't mean we won't ever get hurt, but it does mean the darkness won't

---

[2] George O. Wood, *The Beatitudes* (Springfield, MO: Gospel Publishing House, 2011), 41.

prevail... Because the one who was crucified forgiving his enemies is the King of Glory raised from the dead, Christians believe that no matter what darkness and hate may do, in the end light and love will win."[3] When we faithfully bear the weight of persecution (however it may come), we are demonstrating our belief in Christ's resurrection. We choose to die to self because God brings new life out of our willing sacrifice.

The early Christians understood that in following Christ they would be in direct conflict with some of the most fundamental values of Roman society. Though widespread persecution wasn't always a reality, it was certainly an ever-present possibility. And indeed, there were periodic seasons when it became intense, violent, and systematic. During the latter part of the reign of the emperor Diocletian, for example, thousands of Christians were brutally slaughtered. One of those martyrs, a woman by the name of Euphemia, was arrested for refusing to offer sacrifices to one of the pagan gods. As a result, she was viciously tortured and later killed by a lion in the arena at Chalcedon. Before these events, Euphemia declared: "Both the emperor's commands and those of others in authority

---

[3] Brian Zahnd, Postcards from Babylon (St. Joseph, MO: Spello Press, 2019), 73-74.

must be obeyed if they are not contrary to the God of heaven. If they are, they must not only be disobeyed; they must be resisted."

The early Christians regarded martyrdom to be the ultimate act of loyalty to Christ. Church historian Gerald Sittser points out that "martyrdom demonstrated that the Christian identity took precedence over all other identities, thus testifying that faith was far more important than wealth, fame, and position."[4] This radical allegiance to Christ drew the attention of the pagan world to their message.

SHOWDOWN IN CAPERNAUM

While many Christians throughout history have endured (and continue to endure) extreme cruelty and violence for their fidelity to Christ, persecution doesn't always take the form of bloodshed. Often it emerges in the form of rejection, mockery, and ostracization for those who follow the Jesus way. In his expansion of the eighth Beatitude, Jesus states, "Blessed are you when people revile you and persecute you and utter all kinds of evil against you falsely

---

[4] Gerald Sittser, *Resilient Faith* (Ada, MI: Brazos Press, 2019), 107.

on my account" (Matthew 5:11). This is precisely the relationship Jesus had with many of his contemporaries who were in religious leadership.

After his first brief preaching tour around Galilee, Jesus eventually returns to his home base of Capernaum. As the news begins to spread, the house where he is staying becomes crammed full of people, and is surrounded by a large crowd. Jesus seizes the opportunity and begins to teach. At some point everyone inside the house hears a scraping noise and looks up to see a hole being dug into the roof by a group of men. After a few moments, the men use ropes to lower a mat on which a paralyzed man lies, letting it rest in front of the place where Jesus is standing.

As Jesus observes this unique situation, he looks at the paralytic and declares, "Son, your sins are forgiven." Some of the religious leaders who are present hear this extremely controversial statement and begin to object, "Why does this fellow speak in this way? It is blasphemy! Who can forgive sins but God alone?" (Mark 2:7).

Jesus responds: "Why do you raise such questions in your hearts?" (Mark 2:8). Of course, moments later Jesus stuns the entire crowd by healing the paralytic. But his question to these religious scribes is fascinating. N. T.

Wright translates it this way: "Why do your hearts tell you to think that?"[5]

Somehow Jesus is able to discern that the nature of their objection was not merely intellectual. The dissent originates from within their *hearts* and then takes shape in their minds. Jesus accurately diagnoses that their issues with him go beyond the cognitive level. The root of their opposition is the resistance within their own hearts that is then disguised as a theological concern.

When one begins to embrace the counterintuitive values of the Beatitudes, opposition often comes from well-meaning people, even from among those who profess to follow Christ. And on certain occasions the source of their opposition is not merely intellectual. As with Jesus' antagonists, their *hearts* are telling them what to *think*. The soul-destroying sickness of religious pride affects the way they perceive and interpret the world around them.

Typically in this scenario, no amount of conversation will bridge the divide. In the worst cases, even some of the most astounding works of God (like Jesus healing a paralytic!) will not penetrate hardened hearts. Throughout the story of Jesus, the more he heals people, the more

---

[5] N.T. Wright, *The Kingdom New Testament* (San Francisco: HarperOne, 2011), 68.

intense his opposition. The brighter he shines, the more they hate him. Of course, Jesus loves his critics every bit as much as he loves every other person he encounters. And their resistance to him grieves him profoundly because he sees how sick their souls are.[6] But even Jesus cannot coerce those with stubborn hearts to enter his kingdom.

It takes wisdom and discernment to know when and how to engage honest criticism and when to release an opposing party to God. But following Jesus always leads one through opposition in some form. However unpleasant these experiences may be, we must commit ourselves to the daily habit of prayerfully absorbing God's love, which empowers us to forgive, move forward, and take satisfaction in the opportunity to imitate Jesus. Our willingness to absorb hatred without retaliation renders evil powerless. Most often, this is our most powerful gospel proclamation.

PETER'S JOURNEY

Even people who initially show resistance to the more radical demands of Christ's kingdom can still have hearts

[6] See Mark 3:5.

that are soft and pliable enough to be properly formed over time. This is the compelling story of Simon Peter.

Before he ever meets Jesus, Peter is apparently an enthusiastic supporter of the popular Jewish view that God will someday raise up a militaristic Messiah who will lead a victorious revolution against Israel's enemies. And during his early apprenticeship with Jesus, it is clear that Peter sees Jesus through this lens. Despite all of Jesus' teaching about loving our enemies and blessing our persecutors, it takes a great deal of time for Christ's vision to fully renovate Peter's heart and imagination. Even after moments and seasons of progress, internal obstacles obstruct his spiritual sight. For example, on the road to Caesar Philippi, Jesus poses a very compelling question to his disciples: "Who do you say that I am?" While the other eleven disciples remain sheepishly quiet, Peter boldly declares, "You are the Messiah, the Son of the living God." Jesus responds: "Blessed are you, Simon son of Jonah! For flesh and blood has not revealed this to you, but my Father in heaven. And I tell you, you are Peter, and on this rock I will build my church, and the gates of Hades will not prevail against it. I will give you the keys of the kingdom of heaven."[7]

What an unprecedented moment! Peter must have been overwhelmed with exhilaration at Jesus' blessing. And yet, a mere two verses later, Jesus begins explaining to his disciples that when he later arrives in Jerusalem he will suffer, die, and be raised on the third day. Clearly this image of Jesus enduring suffering and death does not mesh with Peter's preconceived fantasy of a *Braveheart*-style Messiah: "Peter took him aside and began to rebuke him, saying, 'God forbid it, Lord! This must never happen to you.' But he turned and said to Peter, 'Get behind me, Satan! You are a stumbling block to me; for you are setting your mind not on divine things but on human things.'"[8]

Ouch. At this stage in Peter's journey we find someone who is certainly beginning to see things more clearly. He perceives that Jesus is indeed the Messiah whom God has promised through the prophets. And yet it is also painfully obvious that Peter is still terribly confused about the nature of Jesus' mission. He still imagines Jesus victoriously leading a Jewish militia into holy war against the evil Romans. Therefore, when Jesus is later being arrested in

---

[7] See Matthew 16:13-20.
[8] See Matthew 16:21-23.

Gethsemane, Peter takes out his sword and begins to swing it at the arresting soldiers. He doesn't even bother to wait for instruction. For him, this is an act of common sense. He fully expects Jesus to hop on board and begin leading the violent revolt that Peter assumes is inevitable.

Now, perhaps we should give Peter a bit of slack. After all, he has not come up with this mistaken messianic vision on his own. This is how his culture has formed him to think his entire life. His actions are the product of good, conventional, common-sense theology that had been floating around for centuries in Israel regarding the Messiah that God would raise up. There is even plenty of support for this view within the Hebrew scriptures.

Nevertheless, Peter is sorely mistaken. And yet, despite his misplaced rebuke, his repeated failures, his constant misunderstandings, and ultimately his denial, Jesus refuses to give up on Peter. In the days following Jesus' resurrection, Peter returns to his former vocation as a fisherman on the Sea of Tiberias. This is the place where Jesus had said to Peter just a few years before, "Follow me."[9]

---

[9] See Mark 1:17.

And now the resurrected Christ meets him once again on the shore of the sea—only a few days after Peter three times denies knowing Jesus. Now during their discussion on the seashore Jesus asks Peter three times, "Do you love me?" Three times Peter responds, "Yes Lord, you know that I love you." Then three times Jesus replies, "Feed my sheep."[10] Finally once again, just as he did on the road to Caesarea Philippi, Jesus gives another prophecy about Peter: "'Very truly, I tell you, when you were younger, you used to fasten your own belt and to go wherever you wished. But when you grow old, you will stretch out your hands, and someone else will fasten a belt around you and take you where you do not wish to go.' (He said this to indicate the kind of death by which he would glorify God.) After this he said to him, 'Follow me'" (John 21:18-29).

From this point forward we begin to see this amazing shift in Peter's journey. Now that his false assumptions about the nature of Jesus' kingdom have been dislodged, Peter is able to see that the way of Calvary truly is the power of God that transforms the world. This experience so changes him that in his later years, he pens these words to Christians in Asia Minor who are facing imminent

---

[10] See John 21:15-17.

persecution: "Beloved, do not be surprised at the fiery ordeal that is taking place among you to test you, as though something strange were happening to you. But rejoice insofar as you are sharing Christ's sufferings, so that you may also be glad and shout for joy when his glory is revealed" (1 Peter 4:12-13).

Ultimately, at the end of his life Peter himself glorifies God through his own martyrdom. Early tradition tells us that he was crucified upside-down in Rome. This is the same man who decades earlier violently attacked his opposition by swinging his sword against his persecutors. But ultimately Calvary transforms him into a whole new person.

THE REVOLUTIONARY KINGDOM

The genuine expansion of God's kingdom throughout America and the broader Western world will demand that we acquire a more robust theology of suffering. When our sole response to any form of suffering is one of avoidance or aggression, we can be certain that we have strayed from the path of the Beatitudes. Of course, no right-minded person ever seeks to endure suffering simply for its own sake. But there is such a thing as suffering for the *right reasons*. Or to put in Jesus' words, "for righteousness' sake." Bonhoeffer wrote, "Suffering willingly endured is stronger than evil; it is the death of evil."[11]

Pastors and leaders who dare to take our commission of making apprentices of Jesus seriously often walk a lonely road. We have the prophetic task of speaking truth in the midst of a culture of falsehood and pretense. Our efforts will not always result in outward signs of success. In fact, we may even look like failures. People will misrepresent us and malign our character. Nevertheless, our loyalty must remain with Christ, not with our own hunger for human approval. The alternative is a cheap, domesticated brand of consumer Christianity that comfortably acclimates to the dominant society, thus remaining powerless to change the world.

The kingdom Jesus has inaugurated is truly robust, radical, and revolutionary. It is the unstoppable force that prevails against the dark forces that bind humanity in idolatry and injustice. And it advances through those who deny themselves and bear the cross of suffering. We fight not by wielding the sword of power, but by humbly laying our lives down. We fight by loving our enemies, sacrificing

---

[11] Dietrich Bonhoeffer, *Discipleship* (Minneapolis: Fortress Press, 2003), 134.

for the poor, serving the outcast, and swimming upstream in a culture of materialism, greed, lust, and individualism.

As citizens of heaven we live by a counter-cultural vision and set of values, because we belong to a different kingdom. As long as we embody true allegiance to Christ there will always be a price to pay. The kingdoms and powers of the world will not tolerate those who live in uncompromising loyalty to our heavenly King. But Jesus declares that those who are willing to deny themselves and faithfully take up the cross are indeed blessed.

...For theirs is the kingdom of heaven.

REFLECTION QUESTIONS
CHAPTER NINE

1. What image or experience first comes to mind when you encounter the word "persecution?"
2. Why do you think was Jesus perceived to be such a threat to the religious and political powers of his day?
3. How is our willingness to bear the weight of perse-cution an expression of our faith in the resurrection of Christ?
4. Why is being part of a faith community so important when it comes to enduring opposition?
5. What forms of hostility have you encountered in your own pursuit of the Jesus way?
6. If we are to become people who faithfully bear the weight of persecution, what attitude shifts and spiritual practices should we adopt?

AFTERWORD

Like ravens we have gathered around the carcass of cheap grace. From it we have imbibed the poison which has killed the following of Jesus among us.

—Dietrich Bonhoeffer, *Discipleship*

In 1933, Adolf Hitler and his Nazi Party came to power in Germany and began to systematically transform Germany into a totalitarian state. They eliminated all opposition, and all power was consolidated within the Führer himself. From there, he proceeded to implement his nationalistic, militaristic, and racist policies. As part of his agenda, Hitler saw the local churches of Germany as an important ideological battleground. In order to increase and galvanize his influence, he sought to unify all of the Protestant churches of Germany into one state-sponsored, pro-Nazi Church. And thousands of churches and pastors caved in under the pressure.

But from the very beginning there was also a resistance movement. Many churches and their leaders stood in opposition to this development on moral and theological grounds, eventually calling themselves the "Confessing

Church." They recognized that capitulating to the power of the Nazi state would eventually eliminate their doctrinal freedom, corrupt their theology, and compromise their prophetic witness.

Therefore, in May of 1934 these Christians gathered and drafted a document known as the "Barmen Declaration." Against a climate of totalitarian control, the Barmen Declaration was an unmistakable resolution of absolute surrender to the supreme authority of Christ. Through this document, these opposition leaders were issuing a clarion call to the churches of Germany to repent of their cowardice and to pledge their allegiance to Christ, not Hitler.

This prophetic boldness is possible only for those who clearly understand and embrace the gospel announcement of the New Testament. Though we live in a world that is fundamentally broken and beyond human repair, the good news is that God intends to salvage and redeem it. Through his crucifixion and resurrection, Jesus Christ has defeated the powers and principalities that keep the world bound in evil and has now ascended as Lord of all, ruling heaven and earth and making all things new.[1] The Confessing Church

---

[1] See Revelation 21:5.

understood the implications these truths had upon their lives—that God cares about the current affairs of the world, the risen Christ has given us a path we must follow, and our devotion belongs to him who reigns over all. Because the Confessing Church had a deep grasp of these realities, they were able to resist the evils of their generation and embody a faithful witness for Christ.

Now it is our turn. In the midst of the moral darkness of our twenty-first century world, Christians must pledge our allegiance to Christ as our reigning king and embrace his vision for human life and society right now. The people of this world need more than a get-out-of-hell-for-free card. They need a new Master. A new Ruler. A new Teacher who can show us the path that leads to life. His name is Jesus Christ. And everything about our lives must orbit around him.

In the midst of a culture characterized by power-hunger, greed, pride, violence, lust, celebrity-worship, and unbridled ambition, we must live the way our Master taught us to live and trust his agenda for the world right now. Our churches must gather around his teaching and become crucibles of transformation where people are learning how to walk with Jesus on the path of peacemaking, mercy, forgiveness, longsuffering, self-denial, and love of enemies.

As we fully embrace this vision, we may discover that not every churchgoer may actually be interested in being formed in the Jesus way. Nevertheless, our commission remains unchanged. Jesus bluntly told his disciples, "If any want to become my followers, let them deny themselves and take up their cross and follow me" (Matthew 16:24). These are not the words of a slick salesman attempting to bait-and-switch his audience. This is a straight-forward description of the deep-rooted commitment Christ expects all of his apprentices to share. Granted, it would take years for these original disciples to fully understand this calling and live with radical fidelity to Christ. And Jesus was certainly patient with them along the journey. But from the very beginning, he was always leading them towards this trajectory of self-denial and obedience unto death.

Our mission is not to simply secure decisions for Christ in order to save souls for the afterlife. This language would have sounded quite strange in the ears of the apostles, and it bears little resemblance to the content of the message found in the New Testament. Our heavenly task is to be communities of people who are following the path of Christ, adhering to the way of life that he taught and modeled, and leading others in the same.[2] Our primary aim is not to cure social ills. Nor is it to numerically grow our churches. Nor is it to expand our influence over culture. To be clear, these effects are certainly not wrong or evil. In fact, they are often the eventual byproducts of true kingdom advancement. But none of them define the target of our heavenly assignment.

The mission of our churches is quite simply to come under the reign of Christ and learn to walk in his footsteps wherever they may lead us. He is our rabbi. And we are his apprentices who have gathered together to learn his way of life in an age of individualism, consumerism, and secularism. Rather than allowing "isms" like these to pervert our precious faith, may we recapture the radical and subversive character of authentic Christianity encapsulated within the Beatitudes.

I have come to believe that the greatest and most effective witness for Christ in the twenty-first century will not emerge from the stylistic appeal of our worship gatherings. Nor will it emerge from some brilliant outreach program or assimilation strategy (though these may be vital components).

---

[2] See Matthew 28:18-20.

It will emerge from gathered communities of people who have become so thoroughly formed in the way of Jesus, and who have allowed the transformative power of the Holy Spirit to so infiltrate every fiber of their being and every extremity of their lives, that the society around them cannot help but sit up and notice, "These people have been with Jesus."

Made in the USA
Middletown, DE
25 September 2021

48445478R00125